SMOOTHIE
FOR WEIGHT LOSS

200 Delicious Smoothie Recipes That Help You Lose Weight Naturally Fast, Gain energy, and Detox| with 3-Week Weight Loss Smoothie Meal Plan

DORIS M. SMITH

Copyright© 2022 By Doris M. Smith All Rights Reserved

This book is copyright protected. It is only for personal use. You cannot amend, distribute, sell, use, quote or paraphrase any part of the content within this book, without the consent of the author or publisher.

Under no circumstances will any blame or legal responsibility be held against the publisher, or author, for any damages, reparation, or monetary loss due to the information contained within this book, either directly or indirectly.

Disclaimer Notice:

Please note the information contained within this document is for educational and entertainment purposes only. All effort has been executed to present accurate, up to date, reliable, complete information. No warranties of any kind are declared or implied. Readers acknowledge that the author is not engaged in the rendering of legal, financial, medical or professional advice. The content within this book has been derived from various sources. Please consult a licensed professional before attempting any techniques outlined in this book.

By reading this document, the reader agrees that under no circumstances is the author responsible for any losses, direct or indirect, that are incurred as a result of the use of the information contained within this document, including, but not limited to, errors, omissions, or inaccuracies.

Table of Contents

Introduction	1
Chapter 1	
Understanding Your Weight Loss Smoothie	2
Basic Concepts	3
Classification Of Weight	3
The Relationship Between Smoothie and Weight Loss	3
Helpful Tips for Making Your Weight Loss Smoothie	3
Awesome Method to Store Your Smoothies	4
Ingredients for An Awesome Weight Loss Smoothie	4
Health Benefits of Smoothie for Weight Loss	5
Chapter 2	
3-week Meal Plan	6
Week 1	7
Week 2	8
Week 3	9
The Relationship Between Intermittent Fasting and Smoothie	11
Chapter 3	
Breakfast Smoothies	12
Apple with Limey Plumarita Smoothie	13
Delightful Spinach and Raspberry Smoothie	13
Carroty Breakfast Boost	14
Delicious Morning Green Cleanser	14
Superb Popeye's Pride	15
Early Cleansing Smoothie	15
Daily Boosting Smoothie	16
Spinach and Cabbage Morning Plus	16
Cardamon with Gingered Chai Smoothie	17
Icey Blueberry with Stevia Smoothie	17
Grapefruit with Lemony Serum Smoothie	18
Lemony Berry Ginger Smoothie	18
Bright Lemony Cucumber Smoothie	19
Homemade Peter Rabbit Smoothie	19
Berry with Minty Julep Breakfast	20
Classic Reflux Redux Smoothie	20
Simple Slow Fizz Smoothie	21
Easy Pineapple-Celery Smoothie	21
Super Snap Back Smoothie	22
Lemony Cucumber with Apple Breakfast Smoothie	22
Carroty Broccolichoke Smoothie	23
Sunrise Smoothie with Mint	23
Easy Zucchini with Lettuce Smoothie	24
Sweet Asparagus Smoothie	24
Lettuce with Carroty Broccoli Smoothie	25
Garlick with Spicy Spinach Smoothie	25
Apply with Carroty Lettuce Smoothie	26
Carrots with Sweet Beet Smoothie	26
Syrup with Light Berry Smoothie	27
Basil with Spiced Zing Breakfast	27
Tomato Smoothie with Lemony Kale	28
Homemade Mediterranean Smoothie	28
Parsley with Cucumber Summer Breakfast	29
Parsley with Pureed Kiwi Smoothie	29
Classic Veggie Breakfast Smoothie	30
Beet and Celery Delight	30
Chapter 4	
Green Smoothies	31
Classic Kiwi-Cabbage Smoothie	32
Carrots with Garlicky Kale Smoothie	32
Simple Tropical Green Magic	33
Super Easy Greenie	33
Delightful Carroty Green Beast	34
Beet with Spiced Celery Smoothie	34
Asparagus with Spicey Green Shield	35
Mango with Fennel Green Smoothie	35
Mango with Carroty Fennel Smoothie	36
Rhubarb with Kale and Strawberry Smoothie	36
Lemony Avocado with Celery Smoothie	37
Cantaloupe with Carroty Apricot Smoothie	37
Grapy Spinach Smoothie	38
Cold Fruity Green Smoothie	38
Classic Cantaloupe-Veggie Smoothie	39
Flaxseed with Strawberry Smoothie	39
Honeyed Spinach-Berry Smoothie	40
Yoghurt with Milky Peach Smoothie	40
Vanilla with Watermelon Smoothie	40
Chapter 5	
Healthy Diet Smoothies	41
Lemon-Lime Mojito Smoothie	42
Cantaloupe with Limey Melon Smoothie	42
Spinach with Yoghurt-Berry Smoothie	43
Honeyed Banana-Berry Smoothie	43
Cold Minty Yogurt Smoothie	44
Vanilla with Iced Zucchini Smoothie	44
Milk with Sugared Watermelon Smoothie	45
Creamy Gator Smoothies	45
Grapes with Minty Strawberry Smoothie	46
Banana with Gingered Pumpkin Smoothie	46
Icy Berry-Banana with Yogurt Smoothie	47
Milk with Peachy Strawberry Smoothie	47
Iced Blackberry with Banana Smoothie	48
Minty Cucumber Smoothie with Grapes	48
Banana with Spinach-Berry Smoothie	49
Ginger with Carroty Beet Smoothie	49
Classic Hybrid Smoothie	50
Spinach with Vanilla-Apple Smoothie	50
Apple-Berry with Cinnamon Smoothie	51
Lime with Grapy Kale Smoothie	51
Chapter 6	
Weight Loss Smoothies	52
Hot Celery and Carrot Smoothie	53
Simple Kiwi with Berry Freshee	53
Easy Asparagus-Apple Smoothie	54
Carrot with Minty Cucumber Smoothie	54
Carroty Sweet Potato Smoothie	55
Super Easy Veggie Smoothie	55
Simple Reduction Smoothie	56
Apple and Orange-Banana Smoothie	56
Milky Mango with Avocado Smoothie	57
Icey Celery with Carrot Smoothie	57

Fresh Ginger and Strawberry Smoothie	58
Homemade Margarita Smoothie	58

Chapter 7
Detoxifying Smoothies — 59

Lettuce with Minty Apple Smoothie	60
Cucumber with Lemony Cilantro Smoothie	60
Lemon with Sweetened Blueberry Smoothie	61
Spicy Zucchini Smoothie	61
Gingery Collar Green and Pear Smoothie	62
Lemony Cucumber and Iced Apple Smoothie	62
Healthy Beet Smoothie	63
Gingery Cantaloupe Smoothie	63
Succulent Banana and Blueberry Smoothie	64
Superb Ginger Root Smoothie	64
Carroty Clementine Beet Smoothie	65
Classy Spinach with Blueberry Smoothie	65
Chilled Zucchini with Tomato Smoothie	66
Gingered Cantaloupe and Pear Smoothie	66
Chilled Detoxification Smoothie	67
Minty Lettuce and Apple Smoothie	67
Lemony Cucumber and Charcoal Smoothie	68
Limy Cilantro Smoothie	68
Tangy Blueberry Smoothie	69

Chapter 8
Energy Boosting Smoothies — 70

Limy Blackberry and Date Smoothie	71
Milky Berry and Cardamom Smoothie	71
Simple Nut-Milk Smoothie	72
Lemony Banana-Pear Smoothie	72
Gingered Pineapple and Turmeric Energizer	73
Cucumber with Celery Smoothie	73
Revitalizing Banana Smoothie	74
Energizing Banana-Kiwi Smoothie	74
Homemade Celery and Apple Smoothie	75

Chapter 9
Anti-Aging Smoothies — 76

Refreshing Veggie Smoothie	77
Classy Avocado Smoothie	77
Tropical Pineapple Smoothie	78
Soothing Strawberry and Cucumber Smoothie	78
Simple Berry Smoothie	79
Easy Watermelon with Plum Smoothie	79
Anti-aging Veggie Boost	80
Best Hangover Smoothie	80
Carroty Beet Smoothie	81
Lemony Cranberry Smoothie	81
Restorative Broccoli Smoothie	82
Refreshing Potato Smoothie	82
Spiced Veggie Smoothie	83
Delectable Kale and Cucumber Smoothie	83
Minty Plum Smoothie	84
Classical Italiana Smoothie	84
Coconutty Parsley and Apple Smoothie	85
Best Mango and Pineapple Smoothie	85

Chapter 10
Dessert Smoothies — 86

Milk with Chocolaty Frappé	87
Sugary Green Tea Smoothie	87
Limy Mango Smoothie	88
Tasty Banana Shake	88
Perfect Winter Smoothie	89
Best Beet and Berry Smoothie	89
Awesome Spa Smoothie	90
Sweet Cucumber and Berry Smoothie	91
Milky Strawberry Pops	92
Sweet Basil and Greek Yogurt Pops	93
Chilled Jungle Pops	94
Milky Kiwi and Strawberry Pops	95
Delicious Yogurt Smoothie	96
Rich Raspberry Cup	97
Homemade Purpilicious Pops	98
Limy Cherry Smoothie	99
Homemade Honey and Turmeric Latte	100

Appendix 1 Index	**101**
Appendix 2 Measurement Conversion Chart	**104**

Foreword

If you have this book in your hand, it's because you're interested in reaching and maintaining a healthier weight. Following a weight loss diet can be tricky and sometimes require strenuous activities. But do you know you can seat on your rocking chair close to your balcony sipping a nutritious smoothie and eventually lose pounds of weight weekly? It's really that simple!

Our bodies need proper fuel to keep up with the demands of daily activities. It's important that the calories we consume, especially if we're trying to lose weight, gain muscle, or just improve our performance, are quality calories. A protein bar may be high in calories and full of nutrition, but it won't fill you up in the same way a plate of salmon, brown rice and steamed veggies will.

However, you can find an even easier and quicker way around it with smoothies. A good smoothie with protein, healthy fat and whole-food carbs is a great combo for a healthy snack or meal that can promote weight loss.

Smoothies have been found to be great for weight loss and the reason is not far-fetched. When you take smoothies, you will stay full, crave less junk food, and feel like you are eating in a way that is cleaner and lighter. It's such a great feeling that you will always want to feel that way.

In this book, not only will you learn how to incorporate smoothies into your weight loss diet, you will also find a great number of healthy smoothie recipes that will aid your weight loss journey.

Furthermore, you will learn the most important things about smoothie and how it relates to weight loss, you will also become familiar with the different classifications of weight, this will be a beneficial information for your weight loss journey. That's not all, you will also find here some helpful tips for making smoothies.

The smoothie recipes contained in this book will leave you craving for more and at the same time, you will achieve your weight loss goals.

Introduction

Some people say that a smoothie, a day can keep your body pounds away. This is true because when you replace a meal with a smoothie, you can't help but lose weight. Getting a healthy meal in a glass instead of a long sit-down meal full of sugar, salt, and some refined, indigestible meal will always be better for those who intend to shed some weight.

Smoothies are amazing drinks to get you feeling good and a veritable catalyst for losing weight. Moreover, smoothies can be a great way to increase intakes of fruit and vegetables in our diet, which also has many health benefits. It has been proven by people all around the world for generations that certain foods, especially if it is readily digestible, (such as in smoothies), can have a highly beneficial outcome on the human body.

A day's worth of calories includes lots of slow-to-digest fiber in the form of whole carbohydrates, fats, and proteins to keep you feeling full longer. Hunger is kept at bay. When you are not hungry as often, you eat less. When you eat less, you consume fewer calories. When you consume fewer calories, you lose weight. This is the major reason why smoothie is great for weight loss. This information contained in this book will definitely make your weight loss goal s successful one.

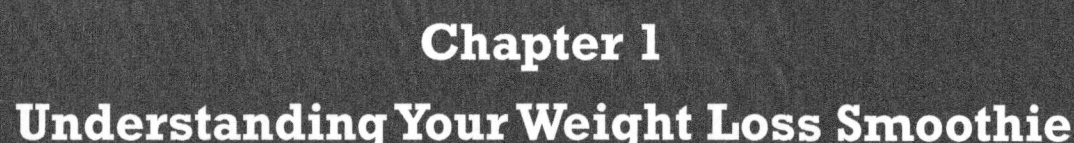

Chapter 1
Understanding Your Weight Loss Smoothie

Smoothie making is a tradition that will never die and there's no need for it to go away. Though smoothies and their ingredients are not cures, and we are not claiming such, it has been discovered that the ingredients used in most smoothies have worked for thousands of people. A bonus is that they are easily digestible and quite delicious. Just what you need to suit your taste bud and loss weight.

In this chapter you will learn some of the most important information about weight loss and smoothies that you need to know. The information here are not exhaustive but they will definitely give you a head start.

Basic Concepts

The followings are the definitions of terms that will aid your weight loss adventure.

1. Smoothies: are blended thick creamery beverage, which have numerous health benefits. Smoothie helps you consume more fruit and vegetables, which are full of antioxidants and nutrients. So, the thing is smoothie is right for your healthy mind and body, as long as you made it from fresh ingredients and didn't forget to eat some whole fruits and milk with it or later. You can drink a smoothie in the morning and have some apples, oranges, or carrots for an evening snack. That will balance your healthy diet.
2. Weight loss: is the gradual reduction of the total body mass of an individual. This can either occur unintentionally because of an underlying illness, or from a conscious effort to improve a perceived obesity state.
3. Overweight: is a body mass index (BMI) of 25 to 29.9 kg/m2 and obesity as a BMI of ≥ 30 kg/m2 . Overweight and obesity are not mutually exclusive since obese persons are also overweight. A BMI of 30 is about 30 lb overweight and equivalent to 221 lb in a 6'0" person and to 186 lb in one 5'6".
4. Body Mass Index: BMI (Body Mass Index) is the most common measure used to define healthy weight. BMI, which describes relative weight for height, is significantly correlated with total body fat content. The BMI should be used to assess overweight and obesity and to monitor changes in body weight. In addition, measurements of body weight alone can be used to determine efficacy of weight loss therapy. BMI is calculated as weight (kg)/height squared (m2). To estimate BMI using pounds and inches, use: [weight (pounds)/height (inches)2] x 703.

Classification Of Weight

Formerly, the index used for the classification of weights was Quetelet, due to technological advancement; the name was changed. This index is used to determine the height and weight of persons. It measures the nutritional values in adults. Individuals' weights are classified to determine the level of fats in the body.

Weight	BMI Class Kg/M2
Underweight	< 18.5
Normal	19 – 24
Overweight	25.0 – 29.9
Obesity	30.0 – 34.9
Extremely Obese	≥ 40

The Relationship Between Smoothie and Weight Loss

Fiber is the key to what makes smoothies such a success when it comes to dieting and weight loss. According to research, people who eat fiber have the lowest body mass index (BMI). Fiber can help keep your digestion working properly, help you lose weight, reduce the risk of heart disease and colon cancer, which lower the dangers of diabetes and stroke. The intake of this high fiber drink will help you flush toxins from your body as well as give you a feeling of fullness, which means that you will naturally want to eat less and lose weight. The bottom line is that smoothie most smoothies contain fiber which makes them one of the major drinks to help you lose weight within a short time.

Helpful Tips for Making Your Weight Loss Smoothie

In as much as you're so eager to hit the blender, it is important you understand the fundamentals of smoothie making. Failed smoothies can lead to frustration and messy kitchens, not to mention wasted food and money. While creating a smoothie isn't necessarily rocket science, there are some tricks and considerations to keep in mind.

1. To get a dripping texture, you need to add half the amount of the liquid first and half at the end.
2. Right after the first liquid is poured into the blender, add powder. Powder thickens and makes your smoothie creamy. When you add your powder early, the powder will blend a lot easier, and you won't end up with a chalky quality.
3. Blend your ingredients.
4. Enables the frozen fruit blend much more efficiently.
5. Always add ice last. This will keep your greens and other foods from overheating and give your smoothie a cool and thick composition.

Awesome Method to Store Your Smoothies

There are many ways you can store your smoothies. But one of the best ways to store your extra smoothie is in a glass container, especially a Mason jar. Use an airtight lid to keep it fresh. Fill it to the very top just to make sure no air gets inside. Professional smoothie makers always add a few drops of lemon juice to their smoothie to prevent it from oxidizing. This method is cost-effective, flexible and require no complex technical competency.

Ingredients for An Awesome Weight Loss Smoothie

Ingredients are the primary building blocks for your smoothie. Understanding your ingredients will help you achieve your weight loss goal. Some of the most common ingredients that you should know about include:

Ingredients	Content/Usefulness
Coconut Water	Electrolytic balance your human blood.
Coconut oil	It contains healthy, healing, medium-chain triglycerides (MCTs).
Raw honey	It's full of vitamins and minerals. Honey works to relieve irritation in your mouth and throat by forming a protective film, making it a great cough medicine.
Turmeric	It equalizes blood sugar levels and is useful for easing stomach cramps and indigestion.
Apple	It reduces cholesterol and enhances mineral absorption.
Macha	It is a natural hormone balancer.
Strawberries	Mild diuretic and a natural painkiller.
Wheatgrass	Minerals and vitamins.
Watermelon	Rich in vitamin A and potassium.
Orange	High in vitamin C and calcium.
Cabbage	Lupeol, sinigrin, diindolylmethane (DIM) indole-3-cardinal (I3C) and sulforaphane.
Celery	Its high concentration of alkaline minerals (especially sodium)
Beet	Full of beta-carotene, calcium, fiber, folate, iron, potassium, protein, and Vitamins B6, C, and K.
Avocado	Full of fiber, folate, magnesium, monounsaturated fat, potassium, steroids (cholesterol-lowering compounds, Vitamin B6, and Vitamin E).
Date	Calcium, fiber, iron, magnesium, manganese, niacin, polyphenols (anticancer compounds), as well as potassium and Vitamin B6.
Pear	Chock-full of vitamins A, B1, B2, C, folic acid, and niacin.

Pineapple	Bromelain.
Bean sprout	Full of calcium, fiber, iron, protein, and sulforaphane (an anti-cancer compound) and Vitamin C.
Carrot	Vitamins B, C, D, E, G, and K, and are rich in beta-carotene.
Corn	Ferulic acid is an anti-carcinogenic compound. It also contains fiber, potassium, and thiamine, as well as lutein

Health Benefits of Smoothie for Weight Loss

While smoothies are widely known to be are beneficial for weight loss. There are also some other health benefits associated with smoothies as listed below:

1. It boosts energy: Coffee and other caffeinated drinks, along with sugary snacks give us these bursts, but they don't last very long. But this weight loss smoothie will give you a steady flow of natural energy that will last for hours.
2. It provides maximum satisfaction: there is always a satisfactorily feeling attached to drinking smoothies for weight loss. It instantaneously quenches your hunger. You won't want to stop gulping this drink.
3. Strengthens the immune system: It helps you to stay healthy and stave off illness. **Strong bones** can be improved with green leaf vegetable smoothies because green vegetables are rich in calcium and vitamin K. All these vitamins are necessary for ensuring calcium reaches your bones but not into body tissues.
4. Detoxified your body: Its leaves a significant impact on your body organs, especially on your skin. It cleanses the liver and stomach. All you need is some fruits like banana, strawberries, blueberries, raspberries, kale leaves, and fish oil.

As you include smoothies into your weight loss diet, you will also get to enjoy some of the benefits listed above. So, you can go wrong with the weight loss smoothies in the following chapters. It's a win win!

Chapter 2
3-week Meal Plan

Smoothie consumption can prove to be very beneficial to weight loss. Smoothies contain high nutritive elements. Drinking smoothies every day is a really great idea especially when your goal is to lose weight. Weight loss is mostly centered on the reduction of calorie intake. The Smoothie recipes in this book will help you reduce your calorie intake and stick to a daily calories range.

These three weeks smoothie meal plan is a combination of various delicious recipes that is worthy of consideration. This plan has been carefully crafted to meet your weight loss goal whether you are a beginner or a long-time smoothie lover.

For three weeks, you will have to drink your smoothies instead of eating your calorie-laden meals. If you don't cheat the process, you will surely benefit and attain your weight loss goal.

Week 1

Creating a calorie deficit is one of the ways to lose weight rapidly. Before you start the first week of meal replacement with smoothie, you need to prepare your body with a three-day detoxification stage. This stage will help you eliminate toxins from your body. The removal of these toxins from your body will help reduce your craving for food and reduce your weight. To detoxify your body, you need to stay hydrated by drinking lots of water in between smoothies. Drinking water will help the detoxify your body quickly. A minimum of 2 liters per day is recommended. After detoxifying, you should gradually introduce smoothies into your meal plan by adding one smoothie into your normal meals daily.

After successfully completing the detox stage, you can then start the first week by replacing two meals daily with fresh and natural smoothie.

While sticking to this diet for the first week, you may get some detox symptoms like headaches, tiredness and feeling sick. This occurs because your body is being deprived from its normal foods and detoxification is taking place. If it persists, you should either slow it down by adding one or two of your normal meals or you stop. This is because this smoothie meal plan is not suitable for long term use, but suitable for a short-term weight loss sprint.

	DAY 1	DAY 2	DAY 3	DAY 4	DAY 5	DAY 6	DAY 7
Wake up	Flaxseed with Strawberry Smoothie (99)	Mango with Fennel Green Smoothie (87.9)	Daily Boosting Smoothie (78.9)	Classic Reflux Redux Smoothie (74.9)	Yoghurt with Milky Peach Smoothie (69.9)	Carroty Sweet Potato Smoothie (45.9)	Lemony Berry Ginger Smoothie (27.9)
Breakfast	Homemade Peter Rabbit Smoothie (86.9)	Delightful Spinach and Raspberry Smoothie (82.9)	Grapefruit with Lemony Serum Smoothie (80.9)	Classic Hybrid Smoothie (76.90)	Super Easy Greenie (68.9)	Easy Pineapple-Celery Smoothie (49.9)	Superb Popeye's Pride (11.9)
Lunch	Lemony Cucumber and Iced Apple Smoothie (84.9)	Milky Berry and Cardamom Smoothie (78.9)	Classic Reflux Redux Smoothie (74.9)	Homemade Margarita Smoothie (73.9)	Yoghurt with Milky Peach Smoothie (69.9)	Carroty Sweet Potato Smoothie (45.9)	Lemony Cranberry Smoothie (38.9)
Afternoon-snack	Classic Cantaloupe-Veggie Smoothie (79.9)	Parsley with Pureed Kiwi Smoothie (77.9)	Homemade Margarita Smoothie (73.9)	Icy Berry-Banana with Yogurt Smoothie (63.9)	Super Easy Veggie Smoothie (41.9)	Carrots with Garlicky Kale Smoothie (31.9)	Classical Italiana Smoothie (22.9)

Dinner	Classic Kiwi-Cabbage Smoothie (74.9)	Cantaloupe with Limey Melon Smoothie (69.9)	Homemade Celery and Apple Smoothie (61.9)	Refreshing Veggie Smoothie (54.9)	Easy Pineapple-Celery Smoothie (47.9)	Delectable Kale and Cucumber Smoothie (37.9)	Sweet Basil and Greek Yogurt Pops (19.9)
Dessert	Milky Strawberry Pops (59.9)	Simple Berry Smoothie (53.9)	Spicy Zucchini Smoothie (49.9)	Chilled Jungle Pops (44.9)	Carrots with Garlicky Kale Smoothie (31.9)	Asparagus with Spicey Green Shield (17.9)	Superb Popeye's Pride (11.9)
Bedtime	Honeyed Spinach-Berry Smoothie (88.9)	Milky Mango with Avocado Smoothie (70.9)	Gingered Cantaloupe and Pear Smoothie (56.9)	Simple Tropical Green Magic (43.9)	Sunrise Smoothie with Mint (39.9)	Lemon with Sweetened Blueberry Smoothie (37.9)	Superb Ginger Root Smoothie (5.9)
Total calories	574.4	522.3	477.3	433.3	370.3	267.3	139.3

Week 2

In the second week, you should never starve yourself because it can sabotage your weight loss goal. Whenever you feel hungry, just make another smoothie. This week is one of the crucial weeks to aid your weight loss goal because your body is gradually adjusting to this new diet. You will need to be disciplined to follow all the recipes in this week. Remember that consistency is the recipe for success in your weight loss goal. If you stick to this plan, you will experience a tremendous change in no time.

	DAY 1	DAY 2	DAY 3	DAY 4	DAY 5	DAY 6	DAY 7
Wake up	Spinach with Yoghurt-Berry Smoothie (87.9)	Delightful Spinach and Raspberry Smoothie) (82.9)	Easy Pineapple-Celery Smoothie (49.9)	Carroty Sweet Potato Smoothie (45.9)	Super Easy Veggie Smoothie (41.9)	Lemony Cranberry Smoothie (38.9)	Classical Italiana Smoothie (22.9)
Breakfast	Easy Zucchini with Lettuce Smoothie (85.9)	Simple Slow Fizz Smoothie (84.9)	Syrup with Light Berry Smoothie (81.9)	Super Snap Back Smoothie (65.9)	Carroty Breakfast Boost (59.9)	Delicious Morning Green Cleanser (46.9)	Sunrise Smoothie with Mint (39.9)
Lunch	Creamy Gator Smoothies (95.9)	Cold Fruity Green Smoothie (86.9)	Revitalizing Banana Smoothie (79.9)	Milky Berry and Cardamom Smoothie (78.9)	Classic Reflux Redux Smoothie (74.9)	Carroty Sweet Potato Smoothie (45.9)	Lemon with Sweetened Blueberry Smoothie (37.9)

Afternoon snack	Delectable Kale and Cucumber Smoothie (96.9)	Grapefruit with Lemony Serum Smoothie (80.9)	Classic Kiwi-Cabbage Smoothie (74.9)	Icy Berry-Banana with Yogurt Smoothie (63.9)	Beet and Celery Delight (42.9)	Chilled Detoxification Smoothie (16.9)	Superb Popeye's Pride (11.9)
Dinner	Tasty Banana Shake (89.9)	Classic Kiwi-Cabbage Smoothie (74.9)	Cantaloupe with Limey Melon Smoothie (69.9)	Milky Strawberry Pops (59.9)	Healthy Beet Smoothie (41.9)	Cucumber with Lemony Cilantro Smoothie (38.9)	Carrots with Garlicky Kale Smoothie (31.9)
Dessert	Grapes with Minty Strawberry Smoothie (91.9)	Delightful Spinach and Raspberry Smoothie) (82.9)	Awesome Spa Smoothie (79.9)	Classic Hybrid Smoothie (76.9)	Cantaloupe with Limey Melon Smoothie (69.9)	Spicy Zucchini Smoothie (49.9)	Classical Italiana Smoothie (22.9)
Bedtime	Homemade Purpilicious Pops (89.9)	Cold Fruity Green Smoothie (86.9)	Sugary Green Tea Smoothie (79.9)	Milky Mango with Avocado Smoothie (70.9)	Minty Plum Smoothie (50.9)	Delectable Kale and Cucumber Smoothie (37.9)	Superb Popeye's Pride (11.9)
Total calories	638.3	580.3	516.3	462.3	382.3	275.3	179.3

Week 3

The third week is about metabolic boosters. Your stomach starts to benefit from your intake of healthy smoothie. The smoothies in this book are healthy and easy to make. Taking healthy smoothies will aid your metabolic process and hence your digestion. The more you take your smoothies, the faster your body reacts positively.

It is important to note that at the end of the third week, you shouldn't just jump on the next available meal you might have missed. You need to gradually include your normal meals into your smoothie meal plan by reducing your smoothie intake the following week.

	DAY 1	**DAY 2**	**DAY 3**	**DAY 4**	**DAY 5**	**DAY 6**	**DAY 7**
Wake up	Simple Reduction Smoothie (85.9)	Milky Mango with Avocado Smoothie (70.9)	Minty Plum Smoothie (50.9)	Easy Asparagus-Apple Smoothie (45.9)	Spiced Veggie Smoothie (31.9)	Cucumber with Lemony Cilantro Smoothie (38.9)	Ging Superb Ginger Root Smoothie (5.9)
Breakfast	Cardamon with Gingered Chai Smoothie (87.9)	Classic Hybrid Smoothie (76.9)	Garlick with Spicy Spinach Smoothie (50.9)	Beet and Celery Delight (42.9)	Basil with Spiced Zing Breakfast (38.9)	Bright Lemony Cucumber Smoothie (21.9)	Parsley with Cucumber Summer Breakfast (15.9)

Lunch	Hot Celery and Carrot Smoothie (94.9)	Cold Fruity Green Smoothie (86.9)	Grapefruit with Lemony Serum Smoothie (80.9)	Iced Blackberry with Banana Smoothie (72.9)	Beet and Celery Delight (42.9)	Carroty Beet Smoothie (37.9)	Chilled Detoxification Smoothie (16.9)
Afternoon snack	Delicious Yogurt Smoothie (89.90)	Parsley with Pureed Kiwi Smoothie (77.9)	Vanilla with Iced Zucchini Smoothie (69.9)	Easy Pineapple-Celery Smoothie (49.9)	Healthy Beet Smoothie (41.9)	Carroty Beet Smoothie (37.9)	Classical Italiana Smoothie (22.9)
Dinner	Fresh Ginger and Strawberry Smoothie (71.9)	Milky Mango with Avocado Smoothie (70.9)	Refreshing Veggie Smoothie (54.9)	Carroty Clementine Beet Smoothie (52.9)	Garlick with Spicy Spinach Smoothie (50.9)	Spicy Zucchini Smoothie (49.9)	Easy Asparagus-Apple Smoothie (33.9)
Dessert	Limy Mango Smoothie (92.9)	Homemade Purpilicious Pops (89.9)	Sugary Green Tea Smoothie (79.9)	Homemade Honey and Turmeric Latte (74.9)	Super Easy Greenie (68.9)	Limy Cilantro Smoothie (38.9)	Sweet Basil and Greek Yogurt Pops (19.9)
Bedtime	Coconutty Parsley and Apple Smoothie (95.9)	Soothing Strawberry and Cucumber Smoothie (75.9)	Ginger with Carroty Beet Smoothie (45.9)	Healthy Beet Smoothie (41.9)	Carroty Beet Smoothie (37.9)	Carrots with Garlicky Kale Smoothie (31.9)	Superb Ginger Root Smoothie (5.9)
Total calories	619.3	549.3	433.3	381.3	313.3	257.3	121.3

Note: The smoothie meal plan above is not suitable for long-term use, but is suitable for short-term weight loss. Peradventure you start feeling drowsy and sickly, you should immediately stop or adjust this plan to fit your individual requirement.

The Relationship Between Intermittent Fasting and Smoothie

Intermittent fasting is one of the fasting lifestyle people engage in for weight loss. This has been a popular fasting method for decades. Intermittent fasting is when people purposedly refrain themselves from consuming high calories within a period of time. Some people choose to engage in intermittent fasting from lunch to lunch or breakfast to breakfast. It all depends on the time that works best for individuals.

The word "fasting" in intermittent fasting is not about starving your body for days or weeks. It simply explains a state when you extend the time you are meant to eat a little longer.

While observing an intermittent fasting, the first meal you will take after depriving your body from its normal foods matter a lot. Most people eat large meals after not eating for hours, which normally backfires. Before they know it, they might develop serious health problems. In order to curb this, it is advisable you break your intermittent fast with smoothies.
Smoothies are healthy blend of fruits and veggies that will help boost your energy and gently introduces nutrients to your body. Its vitamins and minerals are essential elements for keeping the body intact.

To get the most out of your intermittent fasting experience, breaking your fast with a delicious smoothie is one of the healthiest routes to get in shape.
Let the success you have achieved following this meal plan inspire you to live healthy. The recipes in the following chapters will help you set the pace for your weight loss goal. So, let's get you started with some of the best smoothie recipes!

Chapter 3
Breakfast Smoothies

Apple with Limey Plumarita Smoothie
Prep time: 10 minutes | Cook time: 0 minutes | Serves 3 cups

1 plum, seeded
1 green apple, cored and quartered
2 cups spinach
1 cup cabbage
½ lime, peeled

1. Simply puree everything together in your blender.
2. If you'd like to have it a bit thinner, add ¼ cup water.

PER SERVING

Calories: 43.9| Fat: 0.03g | Protein: 0.9g | Carbohydrates: 10.9g | Fiber: 1.9g | Sugar: 7.9g | Sodium: 10.9mg

Delightful Spinach and Raspberry Smoothie
Prep time: 5 minutes | Cook time: 0 minutes | Serves 3 cups

¼ cantaloupe, peeled and seeded
2 kiwis, peeled
1 cup raspberries
2 cups spinach

1. The cantaloupe and kiwis should provide plenty of juice to make the smoothie, but if you'd prefer it thinner, just add a bit of water.
2. Blend all ingredients together and enjoy!

PER SERVING

Calories: 82.9 | Fat:0.1g | Protein: 1.2g | Carbohydrates: 20.9g | Fiber: 3.2g | Sugar: 17.2g | Sodium: 18.9mg

Carroty Breakfast Boost
Prep time: 10 minutes | Cook time: 0 minutes | Serves 3 cups

2 cups broccoli florets
1 cucumber, quartered
3 stalks celery
1 carrot
1 apple, cored and quartered
½ cup water

1. Starting with the broccoli, pulse into small pieces.
2. Slowly add the other ingredients and puree.

PER SERVING

Calories: 56.9| Fat: 0.3g | Protein: 1.9g | Carbohydrates: 12.9g | Fiber: 3.4g | Sugar: 8.5g | Sodium: 38.9mg

Delicious Morning Green Cleanser
Prep time: 10 minutes | Cook time: 0 minutes | Serves 2 cups

1 green bell pepper, de-stemmed
1 cup broccoli florets
1 cucumber, quartered
¼ head cabbage

1. Blend all greens together in the order listed.
2. If you feel it tastes too rich, add a bit more cucumber.
3. All these ingredients work well independently as detoxifiers, but together they create a real powerhouse.

PER SERVING

Calories: 46.9 | Fat: 0.3g | Protein: 2.9g | Carbohydrates: 9.9g | Fiber: 2.9g | Sugar: 4.9g | Sodium: 28.9mg

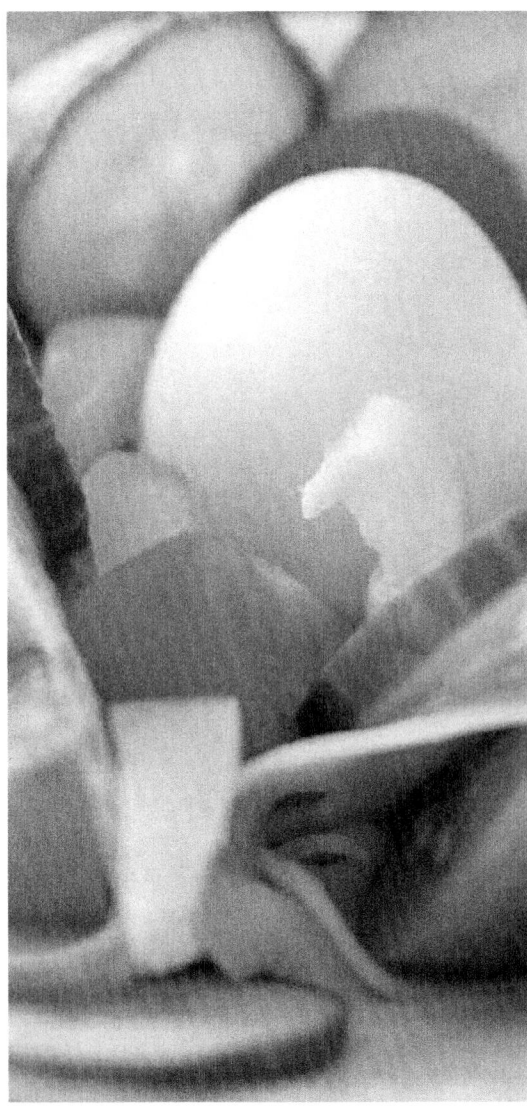

Superb Popeye's Pride
Prep time: 10 minutes | Cook time: 0 minutes | Serves 2 cups

2 cups spinach
½ lemon, peeled
1 sprig parsley
2 stalks celery

1. Just blend all ingredients together until smooth.

PER SERVING

Calories: 11.9| Fat: 0.1g | Protein: 0.9g | Carbohydrates: 2.4g | Fiber: 0.9g | Sugar: 0.9g | Sodium: 37.9mg

Early Cleansing Smoothie
Prep time: 10 minutes | Cook time: 0 minutes | Serves 3 cups

5 broccoli florets
2 green bell peppers, de-stemmed
¼ head green cabbage
½ cup water
2 tomatoes

1. Pulse the broccoli first, then the peppers.
2. Throw in the cabbage and water, and finally the tomatoes.

PER SERVING

Calories: 58.9 | Fat: 0.4g | Protein: 3.4g | Carbohydrates: 12.9g | Fiber: 3.9g | Sugar: 5.9g | Sodium: 36.9mg

Smoothie for Weight Loss | 15

Daily Boosting Smoothie
Prep time: 10 minutes | Cook time: 0 minutes | Serves 2 cups

1 beet with greens
1 carrot with greens
1 apple, cored and quartered
1 inch slice ginger
½ cup water
¼ teaspoon cinnamon

1. Blend all of the ingredients together except the cinnamon.
2. Stir in the cinnamon.

PER SERVING

Calories: 78.9 | Fat: 0.2g | Protein: 1.1g | Carbohydrates: 19.9g | Fiber: 4.3g | Sugar: 13.9g | Sodium: 54.9mg

Spinach and Cabbage Morning Plus
Prep time: 10 minutes | Cook time: 0 minutes | Serves 2 cups

½ clove garlic, peeled
1 celery stalk
1 green bell pepper, de-stemmed
1 carrot
1/8 head cabbage
6 kale leaves
1 cup spinach
1 tomato

1. Blend all ingredients together.
2. If you need more moisture, add ½ cup water.

PER SERVING

Calories: 91.9 | Fat: 0.9g | Protein: 5.9g | Carbohydrates: 18.9g | Fiber: 5.9g | Sugar: 7.9g | Sodium: 86.9mg

Cardamon with Gingered Chai Smoothie
Prep time: 10 minutes | Cook time: 0 minutes | Serves 2 cups

1 cup unsweetened almond milk
1 cup pure pumpkin purée
1 tablespoon pure maple syrup
1 teaspoon grated fresh peeled ginger
¼ teaspoon ground cinnamon
⅛ teaspoon ground nutmeg
Pinch ground cloves
Pinch ground cardamom
4 ice cubes

1. In a blender, combine the almond milk, pumpkin, maple syrup, ginger, cinnamon, nutmeg, cloves, and cardamom. Blend until smooth.
2. Add the ice and blend until thick.
3. Ingredient Tip: Canned pumpkin products are fine but try roasting a pumpkin yourself for lovely flavor and control over additives. Cool any excess pumpkin and freeze it for up to 2 months for future use.

PER SERVING

Calories: 87.9 | Fat: 1.9g | Protein: 1.9g | Carbohydrates: 17.9g | Fiber: 3.9g | Sugar: g | Sodium: mg

Icey Blueberry with Stevia Smoothie
Prep time: 5 minutes | Cook time: 0 minutes | Serves 2

2 cups unsweetened almond milk
1 cup frozen wild blueberries
2 tablespoons cocoa powder
1 to 2 packets stevia, or to taste
1 (1-inch) piece fresh turmeric, peeled
1 cup crushed ice

1. In a blender, combine the almond milk, blueberries, cocoa powder, stevia, turmeric, and ice. Blend until smooth.
2. Substitution Tip: If you are allergic to tree nuts, replace the almond milk with either unsweetened hemp milk or plain rice milk.

PER SERVING

Calories: 96.9 | Fat: 4.9g | Protein: 2.9g | Carbohydrates: 15.9g | Fiber: 4.9g | Sugar: 6.9g | Sodium: 181mg

Smoothie for Weight Loss | 17

Grapefruit with Lemony Serum Smoothie

Prep time: 5 minutes | Cook time: 0 minutes | Serves 2 cups

1 orange, peeled
1 lemon, peeled
1 grapefruit, peeled

1. Blend all three fruits and stir. Enjoy.

PER SERVING

Calories: 80.9 | Fat: 0.2g | Protein: g | Carbohydrates: 20.9g | Fiber: 2.9g | Sugar: 14.9g | Sodium: 0.9mg

Lemony Berry Ginger Smoothie

Prep time: 10 minutes | Cook time: 0 minutes | Serves 3 cups

½ sweet potato
1 handful wheatgrass
½ lemon, peeled
½ cup cranberries
½ inch slice ginger
½ cup water

1. Cut the sweet potato into 1-inch pieces.
2. Blend all ingredients together. The lemon protects it from oxidation, so prepare it in the morning, and bring it along to work.

PER SERVING

Calories: 27.9 | Fat: 0g | Protein: 0.4g | Carbohydrates: 6.9g | Fiber: 0.9g | Sugar: 1.9g | Sodium: 12.94mg

Bright Lemony Cucumber Smoothie
Prep time: 5 minutes | Cook time: 0 minutes | Serves 3 cups

3 lemons, peeled
½ jalapeño pepper, de-stemmed
1 cucumber, quartered
2 cup water

1. Blend all ingredients together. As with many of the others, you can take this one to work with you because the citric acid slows down the oxidation.

PER SERVING

Calories: 21.9| Fat: 0.14g | Protein: 0.9g | Carbohydrates: 4.9g | Fiber: 0.9g | Sugar: 2.4g | Sodium: 5.9mg

Homemade Peter Rabbit Smoothie
Prep time: 10 minutes | Cook time: 0 minutes | Serves 2 cups

1 carrot
2 Kale leaves
1 small cucumber, quartered
1 cup spinach
3 small sprigs cilantro
1 green apple, cored and quartered
¼ cup water

1. Blend all ingredients together in the blender. If it's too thick for your taste, add more water, cucumber, or apple.

PER SERVING

Calories: 86.9| Fat: 0.9g | Protein: 2.9g | Carbohydrates: 19.9g | Fiber: 4.9g | Sugar: 12.9g | Sodium: 47.9mg

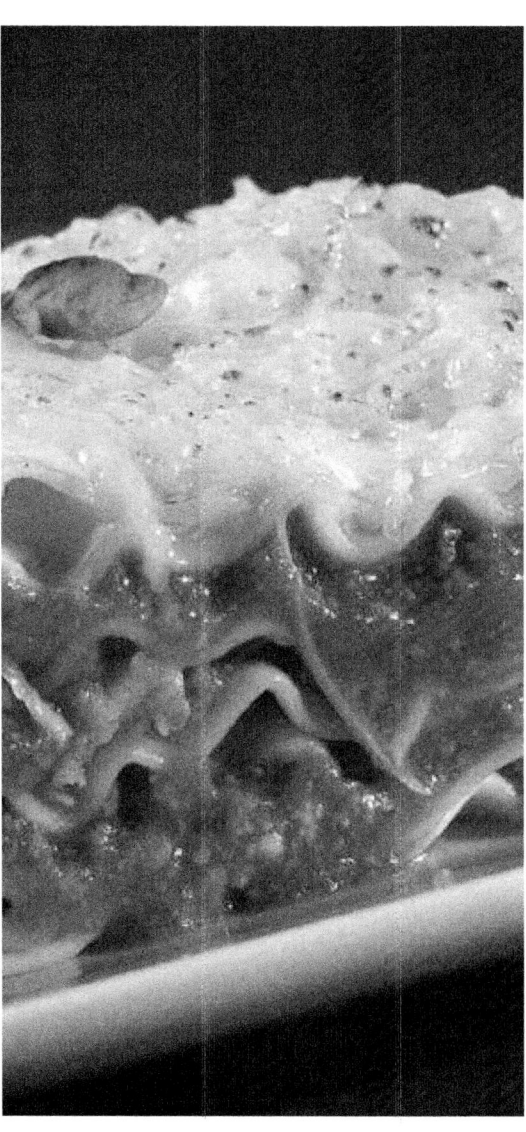

Berry with Minty Julep Breakfast
Prep time: 10 minutes | Cook time: 0 minutes | Serves 2 cups

1 cup cranberries
½ inch slice ginger
1 cucumber, quartered
6 mint leaves
¼ cup water

1. Combine all ingredients in your blender, and pulse until the ingredients are small chunks.
2. Turn up your blender, and puree until it reaches the desired consistency.

PER SERVING

Calories: 87.9 | Fat: 0.3g | Protein: 1.9g | Carbohydrates: 19.9g | Fiber: 0.9g | Sugar: 15.9g | Sodium: 5.9mg

Classic Reflux Redux Smoothie
Prep time: 5 minutes | Cook time: 0 minutes | Serves 2 cups

1 cup spinach
1 carrot with greens
1 banana, peeled
6 mint leaves

1. Blend all ingredients together. You may want to add some water to this just to get a good consistency. Also, ginger works really well here if you'd like to add some.

PER SERVING

Calories: 74.9| Fat: 0.4g | Protein: 1.9g | Carbohydrates: 17.9g | Fiber: 2.9g | Sugar: 8.9g | Sodium: 33.9mg

Simple Slow Fizz Smoothie
Prep time: 10 minutes | Cook time: 0 minutes | Serves 3 cups

2 kiwis, peeled
1 stalk celery
½ inch slice ginger
1 cucumber, quartered
1 apple, cored and quartered
1 cup sour cherries, pitted
½ cup sparkling water

1. Blend all ingredients together and enjoy.

PER SERVING

Calories: 84.9| Fat: 0.3g | Protein: 1.9g | Carbohydrates: 20.9g | Fiber: 3.3g | Sugar: 14.9g | Sodium: 18.9mg

Easy Pineapple-Celery Smoothie
Prep time: 5 minutes | Cook time: 0 minutes | Serves 3 cups

¼ pineapple, peeled
3 stalks celery
1 cucumber, quartered

1. Cut the pineapple into 1-inch pieces.
2. Blend all ingredients together and enjoy!

PER SERVING

Calories: 47.9| Fat: 0.1g | Protein: 0.9g | Carbohydrates: 11.9g | Fiber: 1.9g | Sugar: 7.9g | Sodium: 15.9mg

Super Snap Back Smoothie

Prep time: 5 minutes | Cook time: 0 minutes | Serves 2 cups

1 inch slice ginger
1 carrot with greens
1 apple, cored and quartered
1 lemon, peeled

1. Blend all ingredients together and enjoy.

PER SERVING

Calories: 65.9 | Fat: 0.2g | Protein: 0.9g | Carbohydrates: 16.9g | Fiber: 2.9g | Sugar: 10.9g | Sodium: 21.9mg

Lemony Cucumber with Apple Breakfast Smoothie

Prep time: 5 minutes | Cook time: 0 minutes | Serves 2 cups

1 cucumber, quartered
1 carrot with greens
1 apple, cored and quartered
1 lemon, peeled

1. Blend all ingredients.
2. This one is OK to take with you for lunch, because the lemon juice helps prevent oxidation from taking place.

PER SERVING

Calories: 76.9 | Fat: 0.4g | Protein: 0.9g | Carbohydrates: 18.9g | Fiber: 3.9g | Sugar: 12.9g | Sodium: 23.9mg

Carroty Broccolichoke Smoothie
Prep time: 10 minutes | Cook time: 0 minutes | Serves 2 cups

1 cup broccoli florets
1 artichoke heart
1 carrot with greens
1 clove garlic
1 small cucumber, quartered

1. Blend all ingredients together. You should probably add 1 cup water with this recipe unless you like it really thick.

PER SERVING

Calories: 66.9 | Fat: 0.3g | Protein: 3.9g | Carbohydrates: 13.9g | Fiber: 5.9g | Sugar: 3.3g | Sodium: 105mg

Sunrise Smoothie with Mint
Prep time: 10 minutes | Cook time: 0 minutes | Serves 1

1 cup chopped romaine lettuce
2 medium cucumbers, peeled and quartered
¼ cup chopped mint
1 cup water, divided

1. Place romaine, cucumbers, mint, and ½ cup water in a blender and combine thoroughly.
2. Add remaining water while blending until desired texture is achieved.

PER SERVING

Calories: 39.9 | Fat: 0g | Protein: 1.9g | Carbohydrates: 8.9g | Fiber: 3.9g | Sugar: 3.9g | Sodium: 7.9mg

Easy Zucchini with Lettuce Smoothie
Prep time: 10 minutes | Cook time: 0 minutes | Serves 2

1 cup chopped romaine lettuce
2 medium tomatoes
1 medium zucchini, chopped
2 medium stalks celery, chopped
1 medium cucumber, chopped
½ cup chopped green onions
2 cloves garlic, peeled
2 cups water, divided

1. Place romaine, tomatoes, zucchini, celery, cucumber, green onions, garlic, and 1 cup water in a blender and blend until thoroughly combined.
2. Add remaining 1 cup water, if needed, while blending until desired texture is achieved.

PER SERVING
Calories: 85.9| Fat: 0.9g | Protein: 4.9g | Carbohydrates: 16.9g | Fiber: 5.9g | Sugar: 10.9g | Sodium: 58.9mg

Sweet Asparagus Smoothie
Prep time: 10 minutes | Cook time: 0 minutes | Serves 2

1 cup chopped watercress
1 cup chopped asparagus
1 small lemon, peeled
1 large orange, peeled
1 cup water, divided

1. Place watercress, asparagus, lemon, orange, and ½ cup water in a blender and blend until thoroughly combined.
2. Add remaining water while blending until desired texture is achieved.

PER SERVING
Calories: 64.9 | Fat: 0g | Protein: 2.9g | Carbohydrates: 15.9g | Fiber: 3.9g | Sugar: 9.9g | Sodium: 8.9mg

Lettuce with Carroty Broccoli Smoothie
Prep time: 10 minutes | Cook time: 0 minutes | Serves 2

1 cup chopped romaine lettuce
1 cup chopped broccoli
1 medium zucchini, chopped
2 medium carrots, peeled and chopped
2 cups water, divided

1. Place romaine, broccoli, zucchini, carrots, and 1 cup water in a blender and blend until thoroughly combined.
2. Add remaining water while blending until desired texture is achieved.

PER SERVING

Calories: 70.9 | Fat: 0.9g | Protein: 3.9g | Carbohydrates: 14.9g | Fiber: 4.9g | Sugar: 7.9g | Sodium: 71.9mg

Garlick with Spicy Spinach Smoothie
Prep time: 10 minutes | Cook time: 0 minutes | Serves 1

1 cup spinach
1 medium tomato
1 medium stalk celery, chopped
2 tablespoons cilantro
1 clove garlic, peeled
2 cups water, divided

1. Place spinach, tomato, celery, cilantro, garlic, and 1 cup water in a blender and blend until thoroughly combined.
2. Add remaining 1 cup water while blending until desired texture is achieved.

PER SERVING

Calories: 50.9 | Fat: 0.9g | Protein: 2.9g | Carbohydrates: 9.9g | Fiber: 3.9g | Sugar: 4.9g | Sodium: 65.9mg

Apply with Carroty Lettuce Smoothie
Prep time: 5 minutes | Cook time: 0 minutes | Serves 2

2 cups chopped romaine lettuce
3 medium carrots, peeled and chopped
1 medium apple, peeled and cored
1 cup water

1. Combine all ingredients except water in a blender.
2. Add water slowly while blending until desired texture is achieved.

PER SERVING

Calories: 92.9 | Fat: 0.9g | Protein: 1.9g | Carbohydrates: 22.9g | Fiber: 5.9g | Sugar: 13.9g | Sodium: 66.9mg

Carrots with Sweet Beet Smoothie
Prep time: 10 minutes | Cook time: 0 minutes | Serves 2

1 cup chopped beet greens
2 medium beets, peeled and chopped
2 medium carrots, peeled and chopped
1 medium cucumber, peeled and chopped
2 cups water, divided

1. Place beet greens, beets, carrots, cucumber, and 1 cup water in a blender and blend until thoroughly combined.
2. Add remaining 1 cup water while blending until desired texture is achieved.

PER SERVING

Calories: 96.9 | Fat: 0.9g | Protein: 2.9g | Carbohydrates: 19.9g | Fiber: 5.9g | Sugar: 10.9g | Sodium: 151mg

Syrup with Light Berry Smoothie

Prep time: 10 minutes | Cook time: 0 minutes | Serves 3

1 cup sliced strawberries
1 cup raspberries
1 medium Roma tomato, seeded and chopped
1 cup unsweetened rice milk
1 tablespoon maple syrup
½ teaspoon vanilla
3 ice cubes

1. Combine all ingredients in a blender and blend until smooth. Pour immediately into glasses and serve.

PER SERVING

Calories: 81.9 | Fat: 1.9g | Protein: 1.9g | Carbohydrates: 17.9g | Fiber: 4.9g | Sugar: 9.9g | Sodium: 49.9mg

Basil with Spiced Zing Breakfast

Prep time: 10 minutes | Cook time: 0 minutes | Serves 2 cups

2 green bell peppers, de-stemmed
1 tomato
4 stalks celery
2 basil leaves
½ jalapeño pepper, de-stemmed (optional)

1. Blend all ingredients together and enjoy.

PER SERVING

Calories: 38.9 | Fat: 0.2g | Protein: 1.9g | Carbohydrates: 8.9g | Fiber: 1.9g | Sugar: 4.9g | Sodium: 33.9mg

Tomato Smoothie with Lemony Kale
Prep time: 10 minutes | Cook time: 0 minutes | Serves 3 cups

5 celery stalks
6 basil leaves
1 lemon, peeled
2 kale leaves
1 tomato

1. Blend all ingredients together.

PER SERVING

Calories: 24.9 | Fat: 0.3g | Protein: 1.4g | Carbohydrates: 4.9g | Fiber: 1.9g | Sugar: 1.9g | Sodium: 31.9mg

Homemade Mediterranean Smoothie
Prep time: 10 minutes | Cook time: 0 minutes | Serves 3 cups

½ cup water
1 zucchini
1 cucumber, quartered
1 green bell pepper, de-stemmed
2 sprigs dill
2 springs parsley, plus extra for garnish

1. Add water, zucchini, and cucumber to your blender and pulse. Add the pepper and herbs, and puree.
2. Serve in a bowl and garnish with parsley or pour it in a glass for a hearty meal on the go.

PER SERVING

Calories: 14.9| Fat: 0.1g | Protein: 0.9g | Carbohydrates: 2.9g | Fiber: 0.9g | Sugar: 1.9g | Sodium: 3.9mg

Parsley with Cucumber Summer Breakfast

Prep time: 10 minutes | Cook time: 0 minutes | Serves 4 cups

½ cup water
1 cup broccoli florets
1 tomato
2 sprigs parsley
1 cucumber, quartered
2 cups arugula

1. Combine the water and broccoli in the blender, and pulse until the broccoli is chunked.
2. Add the rest of the ingredients and puree.

PER SERVING

Calories: 15.9 | Fat: 0.2g | Protein: 1.1g | Carbohydrates: 2.9g | Fiber: 1 1g | Sugar:1.9g | Sodium: 8.9mg

Parsley with Pureed Kiwi Smoothie

Prep time: 10 minutes | Cook time: 0 minutes | Serves 2 cups

1 green apple, cored and quartered
2 kiwis, peeled
2 cups romaine lettuce, chopped
2 springs parsley
½ cup water

1. Add all ingredients to your blender and puree.
2. Pour into a glass and enjoy!

PER SERVING

Calories: 77.9 | Fat: 0.4g | Protein: 1.9g | Carbohydrates: 19.9g | Fiber: 3.9g | Sugar: 12.9g | Sodium: 8.9mg

Classic Veggie Breakfast Smoothie

Prep time: 10 minutes | Cook time: 0 minutes | Serves 3 cups

1 cup spinach
1 small cucumber, quartered
2 stalks celery
3 carrots with greens
½ apple, cored and quartered
½ cup water or apple juice

1. Blend all ingredients and enjoy.

PER SERVING

Calories: 69.9 | Fat: 0.3g | Protein: 1.3g | Carbohydrates: 15.9g | Fiber: 2.9g | Sugar: 10.9g | Sodium: 62.9mg

Beet and Celery Delight

Prep time: 5 minutes | Cook time: 0 minutes | Serves 2 cups

1 beet
1 tomato
2 stalks celery
1 cucumber, quartered

1. Blend all ingredients together.
2. Add ½ cup water if you need a bit more liquid.

PER SERVING

Calories: 42.9 | Fat: 0.3g | Protein: 1.9g | Carbohydrates: 8.9g | Fiber: 2.9g | Sugar: 5.9g | Sodium: 50.9mg

Chapter 4
Green Smoothies

Classic Kiwi-Cabbage Smoothie
Prep time: 10 minutes | Cook time: 0 minutes | Serves 3 cups

1 cup cabbage
1 banana, peeled
1 cup strawberries, capped
2 kiwis, peeled
½ cup water

1. Add all ingredients to the blender, and puree until extra smooth.

PER SERVING

Calories: 74.9 | Fat: 0.3g | Protein: 1.9g | Carbohydrates: 17.9g | Fiber: 2.9g | Sugar: 9.9g | Sodium: 11.9mg

Carrots with Garlicky Kale Smoothie
Prep time: 10 minutes | Cook time: 0 minutes | Serves 4 cups

½ cup water
2 carrots
1 tomato
2 cloves garlic
3 kale leaves
½ lemon, peeled

1. Add water and carrots to your blender and pulse a few times to chunk the carrots.
2. Add the rest of the ingredients, and puree until it reaches the desired consistency. Enjoy!

PER SERVING

Calories: 31.9 | Fat: 0.3g | Protein: 1.9g | Carbohydrates: 6.9g | Fiber: 1.9g | Sugar: 2.9g | Sodium: 31.9mg

Simple Tropical Green Magic

Prep time: 10 minutes | Cook time: 0 minutes | Serves 3 cups

3 stalks celery
6 oregano leaves
2 cups spinach
1 cucumber, quartered
1 tomato
6 Brussels sprouts

1. Blend all ingredients together.

PER SERVING

Calories: 43.9 | Fat: 0.4g | Protein: 2.9g | Carbohydrates: 8.9g | Fiber: 3.9g | Sugar: 2.9g | Sodium: 42.9mg

Super Easy Greenie

Prep time: 10 minutes | Cook time: 0 minutes | Serves 2 cups

2 stalks celery
1 cucumber, quartered
2 cups spinach
1 apple, cored and quartered
1 cup water

1. Blend all ingredients together and enjoy!

PER SERVING

Calories: 68.9 | Fat: 0.4g | Protein: 1.9g | Carbohydrates: 15.9g | Fiber: 3.9g | Sugar: 10.9g | Sodium: 42.9mg

Delightful Carroty Green Beast
Prep time: 10 minutes | **Cook time:** 0 minutes | **Serves** 2 cups

1 cup spinach
1 banana, peeled
3 stalks celery
1 cucumber, quartered
1 carrot

1. Blend all ingredients together. This juice packs a nutritional punch you won't find in many other combinations, yet still tastes really good. If you want to spice it up a bit, throw in some black or cayenne pepper after you've poured it in the glass.

PER SERVING
Calories: 84.9 | Fat: 0.4g | Protein: 1.9g | Carbohydrates: 19.9g | Fiber: 3.9g | Sugar: 9.9g | Sodium: 55.9mg

Beet with Spiced Celery Smoothie
Prep time: 10 minutes | **Cook time:** 0 minutes | **Serves** 3 cups

1 carrot with greens
1 yellow beet
2 celery stalks
1 cucumber, quartered
1 green bell pepper, de-stemmed

1. Blend all ingredients together and drink immediately.

PER SERVING
Calories: 35.9 | Fat: 0.15g | Protein: 1.3g | Carbohydrates: 7.9g | Fiber: 1.9g | Sugar: 4.9g | Sodium: 46.9mg

Asparagus with Spicey Green Shield
Prep time: 10 minutes | Cook time: 0 minutes | Serves 3 cups

2 stalks celery
1 green bell peppers, de-stemmed
4 asparagus tips
1 lemon, peeled
1 jalapeño pepper, de-stemmed (optional)

1. Just as you do when you cook it, break your asparagus at the natural break. If you want to spice your smoothie up and gain the benefits of capsaicin, throw a jalapeño into the blender or some cayenne.

PER SERVING

Calories: 17.9 | Fat: 0.02g | Protein: 0.9g | Carbohydrates: 4.4g | Fiber: 0.9g | Sugar: 1.9g | Sodium: 10.9mg

Mango with Fennel Green Smoothie
Prep time: 5 minutes | Cook time: 0 minutes | Serves 4

3 cups of water
1 cup Fennel
1 cup Kale
1 cup Swiss Chard
1 Pear
1 Mango peeled
1 Banana

1. Place fennel, kale, Swiss chard, and the pear inside of the blender.
2. Add the mango, the banana, and water to the combination. Blend everything together until you have liquefied the ingredients.
3. Tips: For this recipe, it is recommended you peel the skin off the mango as the skin is thick and your drink will consist of leathery pieces of mango skin.

PER SERVING

Calories: 87.9 | Fat: 0.4g | Protein: 2.9g | Carbohydrates: 21.9g | Fiber: 3.9g | Sugar: 19.9g | Sodium: 43.9mg

Mango with Carroty Fennel Smoothie
Prep time: 10 minutes | Cook time: 0 minutes | Serves 8

1 cup fennel greens
1 cup kale greens
1 cup Swiss Chard
1 pear
1 mango peeled
1 carrot
3 cups water

1. Put the fennel, kale, Swiss chard, and the pear inside of the blender.
2. Add the mango, carrot, and water. Blend for two minutes until you have reached a smooth texture.
3. Tips: Histidine, an amino acid, found in fennel along with iron help with the treatment of anemia. Iron is the main constituent of hemoglobin while Histidine stimulates the production of hemoglobin and helps with forming other components of blood.

PER SERVING

Calories: 39.9 | Fat: 1.9g | Protein: 4.9g | Carbohydrates: 30.9g | Fiber: 4.9g | Sugar: 0.8g | Sodium: 29.9mg

Rhubarb with Kale and Strawberry Smoothie
Prep time: 5 minutes | Cook time: 0 minutes | Serves 2

2 cups strawberries
1 cup of kale
1 cup of rhubarb
1 cup of water
6 ice cubes

1. Put the ice, kale, rhubarb, strawberries, and water inside of the blender.
2. Puree the ingredients until your drink is a smooth texture free of fruit or veggie lumps.
3. Tips: This drink is known to have a diuretic effect, so it is recommended to drink this beverage when you are at a place that has a restroom nearby or home.

PER SERVING

Calories: 78.9 | Fat: 0.9g | Protein: 4.9g | Carbohydrates: 33.9g | Fiber: 7.9g | Sugar: 6.9g | Sodium: 45.9mg

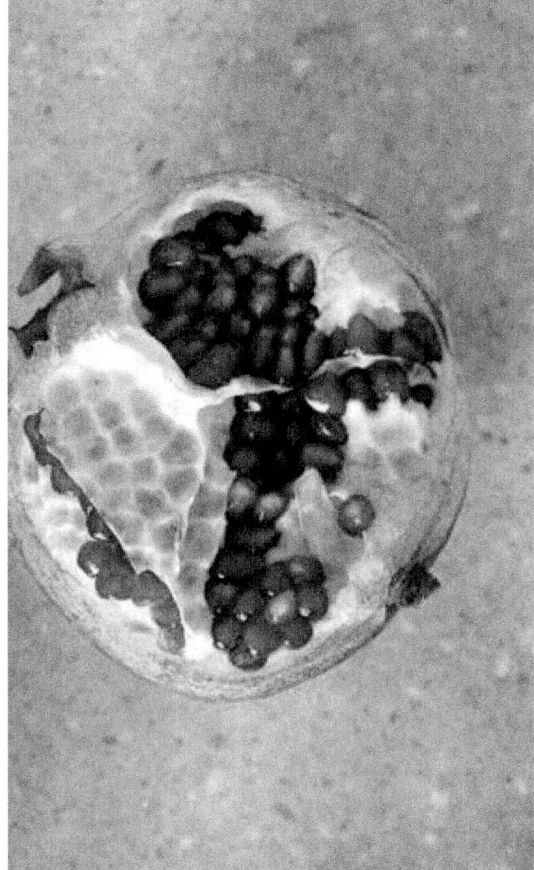

Lemony Avocado with Celery Smoothie

Prep time: 15 minutes | Cook time: 0 minutes | Serves 3

2 large tomatoes
1 large cucumber
3 cups of spinach or baby greens mix
½ lemon
½ red bell pepper
¼ avocado
1 stalk of celery
½ cup water

1. Place the tomatoes, cucumber, spinach, and the lemon in the blender.
2. Next, add the pepper, avocado, the celery, and water to the rest of the ingredients.
3. Puree for 3 minutes and enjoy.
4. Tips: Leave the cucumber skin on for this recipe.

PER SERVING

Calories: 77.9 | Fat: 2.9g | Protein: 2.9g | Carbohydrates: 11.9g | Fiber: 3.9g | Sugar: 5.3g | Sodium: 38.9mg

Cantaloupe with Carroty Apricot Smoothie

Prep time: 7 minutes | Cook time: 0 minutes | Serves 3

1 tablespoon spirulina
1 cup of spinach
1 cup of asparagus
2 apricots
½ of cantaloupe
2 carrots
½ cup of water

1. Put the cantaloupe and apricots in first to make a fruity base.
2. Then add carrots, asparagus, spinach, and spirulina to mix with the ingredients.
3. Finally, pour the water over everything and blend on high for 2 minutes.
4. Tips: It is best to blend the spinach with the carrots and asparagus to help get the most out of the leafy vegetable when mixing.

PER SERVING

Calories: 55.9 | Fat: 0.4g | Protein: 3.9g | Carbohydrates: 10.9g | Fiber: 2.9g | Sugar: 2.9g | Sodium: 74.9mg

Grapy Spinach Smoothie
Prep time: 5 minutes | Cook time: 0 minutes | Serves 2

½ cup of cranberries
1 apple
1 cup grapes
2 cups of spinach
1 stalk of celery
8 oz of water

1. First blend the water, spinach, and celery to make your liquid vegetable base.
2. Add all the fruits and blend on high for 3 minutes. Make sure that the smoothie has no chunks. Serve and enjoy this delicious drink.
3. Tips: Cranberries are rank 33 out of 100 for potential pesticide residue according to research conducted by the Environmental Working Group (EWG). Make sure to wash the cranberries off thoroughly if you are not using organic cranberries.

PER SERVING
Calories: 96.9 | Fat: 0.2g | Protein: 1.1g | Carbohydrates: 24.9g | Fiber: 4.4g | Sugar: 13.9g | Sodium: 35.9mg

Cold Fruity Green Smoothie
Prep time: 5 minutes | Cook time: 0 minutes | Serves 5

3 cups cold water
3 cups leafy greens, packed
3 cups fresh and frozen fruit

1. Turn on your blender
2. Blend all ingredients on high for 30 to 45 seconds, or until desired consistency is reached.

PER SERVING
Calories: 86.9 | Fat: 0g | Protein: 0.9g | Carbohydrates: 16.9g | Fiber: 1.9g | Sugar: 12.9g | Sodium: 31.9mg

Classic Cantaloupe-Veggie Smoothie

Prep time: 5 minutes | Cook time: 0 minutes | Serves 5

2 cups cantaloupe diced
1 cup frozen pineapple chunks
½ banana
2 carrots halved
1 ½ cups water
1 tomato
1 tablespoon agave nectar (or your choice of sweetener, to taste)

1. Turn on your blender
2. Blend all ingredients on high for 30 to 45 seconds, or until desired consistency is reached.

PER SERVING

Calories: 76.9 | Fat: 0g | Protein: 0.9g | Carbohydrates: 18.9g | Fiber: 1.9g | Sugar: 14.9g | Sodium: 27.9mg

Flaxseed with Strawberry Smoothie

Prep time: 10 minutes | Cook time: 0 minutes | Serves 3

6 fl. oz. coconut milk
1 cup fresh strawberries
2 tbsp. flaxseeds
1 Greek yogurt vanilla or coconut flavor (5.3 oz.)
½ teaspoon stevia (1 packet)
1 cup ice cubes

1. Turn on your blender
2. Blend all ingredients on high for 30 to 45 seconds, or until desired consistency is reached.

PER SERVING

Calories: 99 | Fat: 2.9g | Protein: 6.9g | Carbohydrates: 10.9g | Fiber: 1.9g | Sugar: 8.9g | Sodium: 59.9mg

Honeyed Spinach-Berry Smoothie
Prep time: 10 minutes | Cook time: 0 minutes | Serves 5

2 cups almond milk
1 banana
½ cup fresh raspberries
5 fresh strawberries
2 tablespoon honey
2 cups ice cubes
1 orange peeled and halved
3 cups spinach

1. Turn on your blender
2. Blend all ingredients on high for 30 to 45 seconds, or until desired consistency is reached.

PER SERVING

Calories: 88.9 | Fat: 0.9g | Protein: 0.9g | Carbohydrates: 18.9g | Fiber: 2.9g | Sugar: 12.9g | Sodium: 85.9mg

Yoghurt with Milky Peach Smoothie
Prep time: 5 minutes | Cook time: 0 minutes | Serves 4

6 fl. oz. low-fat milk (or your choice of milk)
3 fresh peaches peeled & pitted
2 cups ice cubes
½ cup fat-free peach yogurt

1. Turn on your blender
2. Blend all ingredients on high for 30 to 45 seconds, or until desired consistency is reached.
3. Notes: For a unique peach flavor, add ¼ tsp of nutmeg to spice up your smoothie.

PER SERVING

Calories: 69.9 | Fat: 0g | Protein: 3.9g | Carbohydrates: 12.9g | Fiber: 0.9g | Sugar: 10.9g | Sodium: 39.9mg

Vanilla with Watermelon Smoothie
Prep time: 5 minutes | Cook time: 0 minutes | Serves 2

1 scoop whey protein powder, vanilla
3 cups watermelon
1 cup ice

1. Blend ingredients in a blender.
2. Divide into two glasses and serve.

PER SERVING

Calories: 92.9 | Fat: 0.9g | Protein: 7.9g | Carbohydrates: 12.9g | Fiber: 0.9g | Sugar: 13.9g | Sodium: 55.9mg

Chapter 5
Healthy Diet Smoothies

Lemon-Lime Mojito Smoothie
Prep time: 10 minutes | Cook time: 0 minutes | Serves 4

3 cups ice cubes, or as desired
1 orange, peeled and segmented
2 cups baby spinach leaves, or to taste
10 fresh mint leaves, or more to taste
1 (7 ounce) can crushed pineapple
1 lemon, juiced
½ cup water, or to taste
1 lime, juiced
1 banana, broken into chunks

1. Blend ice, spinach, pineapple, water, banana, orange, mint, lemon juice, and lime juice in a blender until smooth.

PER SERVING

Calories: 93.9 | Fat: 0.2g | Protein: 1.4g | Carbohydrates: 23.9g | Fiber: 2.3g | Sugar: 1.9g | Sodium: 15.9mg

Cantaloupe with Limey Melon Smoothie
Prep time: 5 minutes | Cook time: 0 minutes | Serves 4

¼ cantaloupe - peeled, seeded, and cubed
¼ honeydew melon - peeled, seeded, and cubed
1 lime, juiced
2 tablespoons sugar

1. In a blender, combine cantaloupe, honeydew, lime juice and sugar. Blend until smooth.
2. Pour into glasses and serve.

PER SERVING

Calories: 69.9 | Fat: 0.1g | Protein: 0.9g | Carbohydrates: 17.9g | Fiber: 0.0g | Sugar: 3.9g | Sodium: 0.9mg

Spinach with Yoghurt-Berry Smoothie

Prep time: 10 minutes | Cook time: 0 minutes | Serves 4

2 cups frozen berries
¼ cup fresh spinach, or to taste
1 cup plain yogurt
5 strawberries
½ cup orange juice

1. Blend berries, yogurt, orange juice, spinach, and strawberries together in a blender until smooth.

PER SERVING

Calories: 87.9 | Fat: 16.9g | Protein: 3.9g | Carbohydrates: 16.9g | Fiber: 0.9g | Sugar: 2.9g | Sodium: 4.9mg

Honeyed Banana-Berry Smoothie

Prep time: 5 minutes | Cook time: 0 minutes | Serves 4

4 cups ice
1 cup orange juice
1 cup strawberries
2 tablespoons honey
½ banana

1. 1. Blend the ice, strawberries, banana, orange juice, and honey in a blender until smooth.

PER SERVING

Calories: 84.9 | Fat: 0.2g | Protein: 0.9g | Carbohydrates: 20.9g | Fiber: 1.9g | Sugar: 9.9g | Sodium: 5.9mg

Cold Minty Yogurt Smoothie

Prep time: 7 minutes | Cook time: 0 minutes | Serves 4

1 cup plain yogurt
3 cups cold water
1 mango - peeled, seeded, and chopped
1 pinch salt
1 tablespoon white sugar
4 sprigs fresh mint, garnish

1. In a blender, combine yogurt, mango, sugar, water, and salt.
2. Blend until smooth. Pour into glasses and serve garnished with a sprig of mint.

PER SERVING

Calories: 84.9 | Fat: 0.9g | Protein: 3.9g | Carbohydrates: 15.9g | Fiber: 0g | Sugar: 1.9g | Sodium: 80.9mg

Vanilla with Iced Zucchini Smoothie

Prep time: 5 minutes | Cook time: 0 minutes | Serves 2

1 zucchini, cubed
2 tablespoons granular sucralose sweetener (such as Splenda)
5 ice cubes
¾ teaspoon vanilla extract
1 cup orange juice

1. Place the zucchini, ice cubes, orange juice, sweetener, and vanilla extract into a blender.
2. Cover, and blend until smooth, about 1 minute.

PER SERVING

Calories: 69.9 | Fat: 0.3g | Protein: 1.9g | Carbohydrates: 14.9g | Fiber: 1.9g | Sugar: 0.9g | Sodium: 0mg

Milk with Sugared Watermelon Smoothie

Prep time: 10 minutes | Cook time: 0 minutes | Serves 4

1 ½ cups diced watermelon
2 ¼ cups milk
2 teaspoons white sugar

1. Process the watermelon and milk together in a blender until smooth.
2. Add the sugar and blend another 10 seconds to incorporate.
3. Serve immediately.

PER SERVING

Calories: 93.9 | Fat: 2.9g | Protein: 4.9g | Carbohydrates: 12.9g | Fiber: 0.1g | Sugar: 10.9g | Sodium: 72.9mg

Creamy Gator Smoothies

Prep time: 5 minutes | Cook time: 0 minutes | Serves 2

2 cups ice
2 cups grape flavored sports drink
2 scoops vanilla ice cream

1. In a blender, combine ice, sports drink and ice cream.
2. Blend until smooth.
3. Pour into glasses and serve.

PER SERVING

Calories: 95.9 | Fat: 1.9g | Protein: 0.9g | Carbohydrates: 17.9g | Fiber: 0.2g | Sugar: 0.0g | Sodium: 2.9mg

Grapes with Minty Strawberry Smoothie

Prep time: 10 minutes | Cook time: 0 minutes | Serves 2

¼ cup red seedless grapes, frozen
3 frozen strawberries
¼ cup unsweetened applesauce, or to taste
1 cup cubed fresh pineapple
1 tablespoon fresh lime juice
3 fresh mint leaves

1. Place frozen grapes, applesauce, and lime juice into a blender.
2. Puree until smooth. Add frozen strawberries, cubed pineapple, and mint leaves.
3. Pulse a few times until the strawberries and pineapple are in small bits.

PER SERVING

Calories: 91.9 | Fat: 0.2g | Protein: 0.9g | Carbohydrates: 23.9g | Fiber: 0.9g | Sugar: 8.9g | Sodium: 0.9mg

Banana with Gingered Pumpkin Smoothie

Prep time: 5 minutes | Cook time: 0 minutes | Serves 2

8 ice cubes, or as desired
¼ cup pumpkin puree
1 banana
1/8 teaspoon ground cinnamon
¼ cup yogurt
1 pinch ground ginger

1. Blend ice cubes, banana, yogurt, pumpkin, cinnamon, and ginger together in a blender until smooth.

PER SERVING

Calories: 83.9 | Fat: 0.9g | Protein: 2.9g | Carbohydrates: 18.9g | Fiber: 0.9g | Sugar: 1.9g | Sodium: 15.9mg

Icy Berry-Banana with Yogurt Smoothie

Prep time: 10 minutes | Cook time: 0 minutes | Serves 4

1 cup frozen blueberries
½ cup water
½ cup sliced banana
½ cup vanilla yogurt
½ cup sliced peeled cucumber
½ cup crushed ice, or as needed

1. Blend blueberries, banana, cucumber, water, and yogurt together in a blender until smooth.
2. Add crushed ice and blend until smooth.

PER SERVING

Calories: 63.9 | Fat: 0.9g | Protein: 1.9g | Carbohydrates: 13.9g | Fiber: 0.9g | Sugar: 7.9g | Sodium: 1.9mg

Milk with Peachy Strawberry Smoothie

Prep time: 5 minutes | Cook time: 0 minutes | Serves 2

½ cup frozen peach slices
½ cup frozen strawberries
¼ cup milk
½ cup ice cubes

1. 1. In a blender, blend the peaches, strawberries, milk, and ice cubes until smooth.

PER SERVING

Calories: 92.9 | Fat: 0.9g | Protein: 1.9g | Carbohydrates: 21.9g | Fiber: 0.9g | Sugar: 3.9g | Sodium: 13.9mg

Iced Blackberry with Banana Smoothie
Prep time: 10 minutes | Cook time: 0 minutes | Serves 4

1 cup fresh blackberries, or more to taste
2 cups crushed ice
5 large strawberries, hulled and halved
1 teaspoon white sugar, or to taste (optional)
1 large banana
12 fresh blackberries
1/3 cup orange juice

1. Place 1 cup blackberries, strawberries, banana, orange juice, and ice into a blender in that order, and blend on high speed until smooth, 30 seconds to 1 minute.
2. Pour into 4 glasses and top each serving with 3 blackberries for garnish.

PER SERVING

Calories: 72.9 | Fat: 0.4g | Protein: 1.3g | Carbohydrates: 17.9g | Fiber: 2.9g | Sugar: 4.9g | Sodium: 2.9mg

Minty Cucumber Smoothie with Grapes
Prep time: 10 minutes | Cook time: 0 minutes | Serves 4

3 cups honeydew melon - peeled, seeded, and cubed
1 cucumber, peeled and chopped
3 cups ice cubes
½ cup broccoli florets (optional)
1 cup green grapes
1 sprig fresh mint

1. Place the honeydew melon, ice cubes, grapes, cucumber, broccoli, and mint into a blender.
2. Cover, and puree until smooth.

PER SERVING

Calories: 85.9 | Fat: 0.4g | Protein: 1.9g | Carbohydrates: 20.9g | Fiber: 0.9g | Sugar: 10.9g | Sodium: 29.9mg

Banana with Spinach-Berry Smoothie
Prep time: 10 minutes | Cook time: 0 minutes | Serves 4

1 cup fresh strawberries
2 cups fresh baby spinach
1 banana
1 cup ice
1 cup orange juice
4 (3.5 gram) packets Truvia natural sweetener, or more to desired level of sweetness 1 cup almond milk

1. 1. Add all ingredients into a blender.
2. 2. Blend on high until smooth.

PER SERVING

Calories: 85.9 | Fat: 0.9g | Protein: 1.9g | Carbohydrates: 21.9g | Fiber: 1.9g | Sugar: 8.9g | Sodium: 37.9mg

Ginger with Carroty Beet Smoothie
Prep time: 10 minutes | Cook time: 0 minutes | Serves 2

1 carrot
½ beet (chopped)
1 celery stalk (chopped)
½ cucumber (peeled and sliced)
1 tablespoons of sliced ginger
1 cup ice cubes
½ cup spring water

1. Turn on your blender
2. Blend all ingredients on high for 30 -45 seconds, or until desired consistency is reached.

PER SERVING

Calories: 45.9 | Fat: 0.2g | Protein: 1.4g | Carbohydrates: 9.9g | Fiber: 1.9g | Sugar: 2.9g | Sodium: 52.9mg

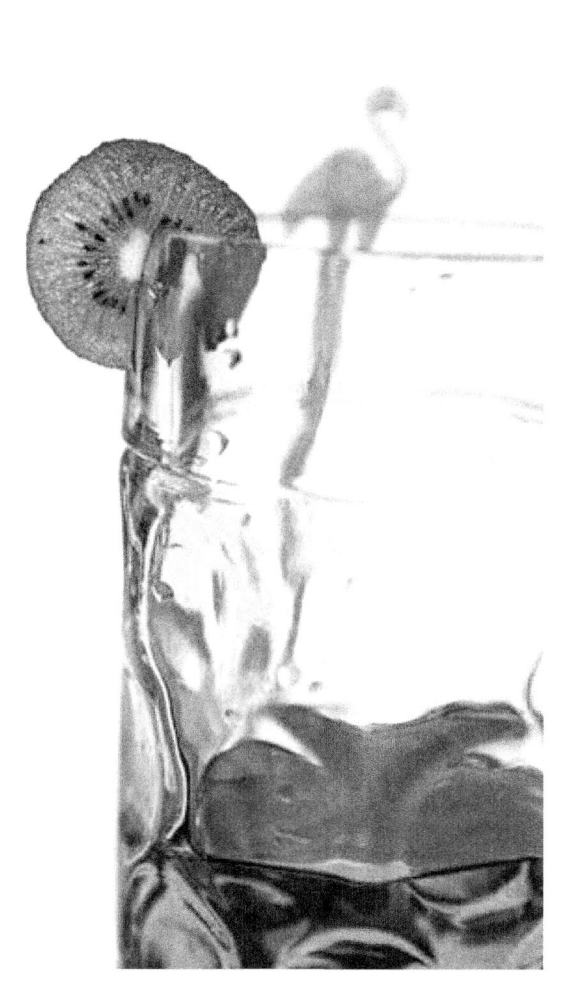

Classic Hybrid Smoothie
Prep time: 10 minutes | Cook time: 0 minutes | Serves 2

½ cup spring water
½ cup orange juice
½ cup strawberries
½ cup blueberries
1 cup kale or spinach (chopped)

1. Turn on your blender
2. Blend all ingredients on high for 30 -45 seconds, or until desired consistency is reached.

PER SERVING

Calories: 76.9 | Fat: 0.3g | Protein: 1.9g | Carbohydrates: 17.9g | Fiber: 1.9g | Sugar: 9.9g | Sodium: 12.9mg

Spinach with Vanilla-Apple Smoothie
Prep time: 10 minutes | Cook time: 0 minutes | Serves 2

2 apples, cored and peeled
¼ teaspoon nutmeg
½ teaspoon cinnamon
½ cup blueberries
2 cups spinach, raw
2 cups of water
2 teaspoons vanilla extract

1. Add listed ingredients to a blender
2. Blend until you have a smooth and creamy texture
3. Serve chilled and enjoy!

PER SERVING

Calories: 81.9 | Fat: 0.4g | Protein: 0.9g | Carbohydrates: 18.9g | Fiber: 1.9g | Sugar: 4.9g | Sodium: 29.9mg

Apple-Berry with Cinnamon Smoothie
Prep time: 10 minutes | **Cook time:** 0 minutes | **Serves 2**

2 apples, cored and peeled
¼ teaspoon nutmeg
½ teaspoon cinnamon
½ cup blueberries
2 cups spinach, raw
2 cups of water
2 teaspoons vanilla extract

1. Add listed ingredients to a blender
2. Blend until you have a smooth and creamy texture
3. Serve chilled and enjoy!

PER SERVING

Calories: 81.9 | Fat: 0g | Protein: 0.9g | Carbohydrates: 18.9g | Fiber: 6.9g | Sugar: 13.9g | Sodium: 32.9mg

Lime with Grapy Kale Smoothie
Prep time: 10 minutes | **Cook time:** 0 minutes | **Serves 4**

4 cups fresh kale, chopped
2 cups seedless green grapes
3 cups water
½ cup ice cubes
4 drops stevia
2 tablespoons fresh lime juice

1. Add everything in a food processor and pulse until smooth.
2. Pour in serving glasses.
3. Top with crushed ice.
4. Serve with a smile.

PER SERVING

Calories: 90.9 | Fat: 0g | Protein: 2.5g | Carbohydrates: 22.6g | Fiber: 1.5g | Sugar: 10.9g | Sodium: 18.9mg

Chapter 6
Weight Loss Smoothies

Hot Celery and Carrot Smoothie
Prep time: 10 minutes | Cook time: 0 minutes | Serves 2

½ cup apple juice
1 cup tomato juice
1 ½ cups chopped tomatoes
2/3 cups chopped carrots
2/3 cups chopped celery
2/3 teaspoons hot sauce
9 ice cubes

1. Add listed ingredients to a blender
2. Blend all ingredients on high for 45 seconds, or until desired consistency is reached.

PER SERVING

Calories: 94.9 | Fat: 0.4g | Protein: 2.9g | Carbohydrates: 21.9g | Fiber: 3.9g | Sugar: 13.9g | Sodium: 461mg

Simple Kiwi with Berry Freshee
Prep time: 10 minutes | Cook time: 0 minutes | Serves 4

1 banana, peeled
5 strawberries, capped, plus 1 strawberry for garnish
¼ cup blueberries
4 kiwis, peeled
1 small cucumber, quartered
¼ cup water

1. Toss all ingredients in your blender and puree until smooth.
2. Pour into glass and garnish with a strawberry.

Per Serving

Calories: 71.9 | Fat: 0.3g | Protein: 1.9g | Carbohydrates: 17.9g | Fiber: 2.3g | Sugar: 10.9g | Sodium: 4.9mg

Easy Asparagus-Apple Smoothie
Prep time: 10 minutes | Cook time: 0 minutes | Serves 4

1 green apple, cored and quartered
6 asparagus tips
2 cups spinach
1 cucumber, quartered
½ cup water

1. Add the apple and asparagus to the blender, and pulse until they are in chunks.
2. Toss in the remaining ingredients, and puree until it reaches the desired texture.
3. This one may be a little chewy and will keep you full for hours.

PER SERVING

Calories: 33.9 | Fat: 0.12g | Protein: 0.9g | Carbohydrates: 7.9g | Fiber: 1.9g | Sugar: 5.9g | Sodium: 13.9mg

Carrot with Minty Cucumber Smoothie
Prep time: 5 minutes | Cook time: 0 minutes | Serves 2

1 carrot with greens
1 green apple, cored and quartered
½ cup water
1 small cucumber, quartered
6 mint leaves

1. Blend the carrot, apple, and water on the "chop" setting, then toss in the cucumber and mint leaves.
2. Puree to the consistency you prefer.

PER SERVING

Calories: 75.9 | Fat: 0.4g | Protein: 1.9g | Carbohydrates: 17.9g | Fiber: 3.9g | Sugar: 11.9g | Sodium: 25.9mg

Carroty Sweet Potato Smoothie

Prep time: 10 minutes | Cook time: 0 minutes | Serves 3

1 small, sweet potato
1 beet, with or without greens
1 carrot with greens
1 cucumber, quartered

1. Cut the sweet potato into 1-inch cubes.
2. Pulse your sweet potato and beet first, then add the carrot and cucumber.
3. Once you get past the fact that the taste doesn't match the color, you'll really enjoy this juice!

PER SERVING

Calories: 45.9 | Fat: 0.13g | Protein: 1.3g | Carbohydrates: 9.9g | Fiber: 2.4g | Sugar: 4.9g | Sodium: 43.9mg

Super Easy Veggie Smoothie

Prep time: 10 minutes | Cook time: 0 minutes | Serves 3

1 clove garlic
¼ head cabbage
1 kale leaf
1 beet
1 carrot
1 stalk celery
1 cup water

1. Add all ingredients and blend.
2. If you'd like, add a pinch or two of sea salt for flavor and a mineral boost, or perhaps cayenne for the extra antioxidant pop from the capsaicin.

PER SERVING

Calories: 41.9 | Fat: 0.2g | Protein: 1.9g | Carbohydrates: 8.9g | Fiber: 2.9g | Sugar: 4.9g | Sodium: 57.9mg

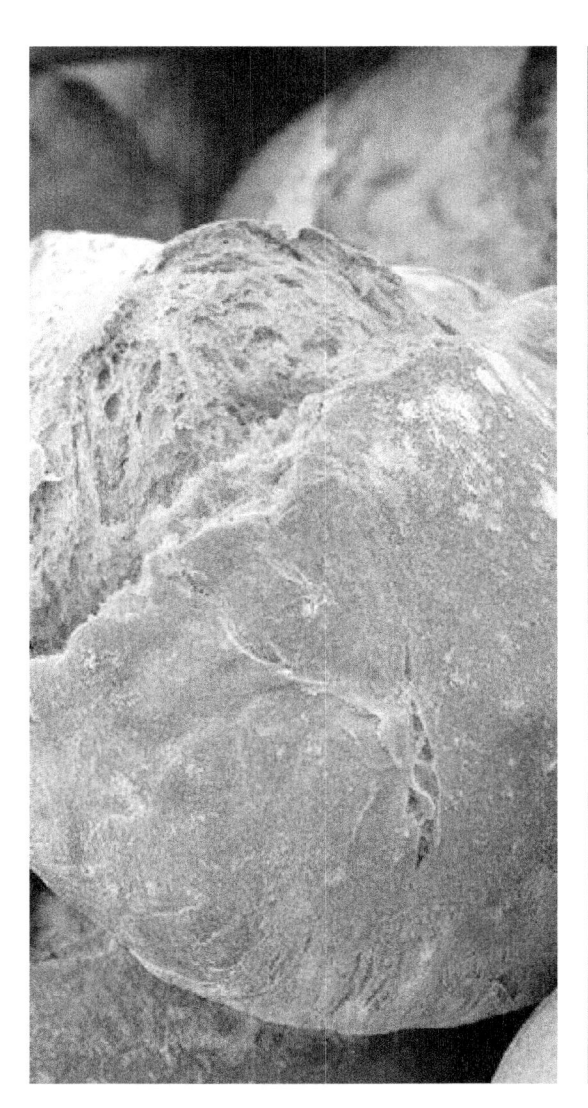

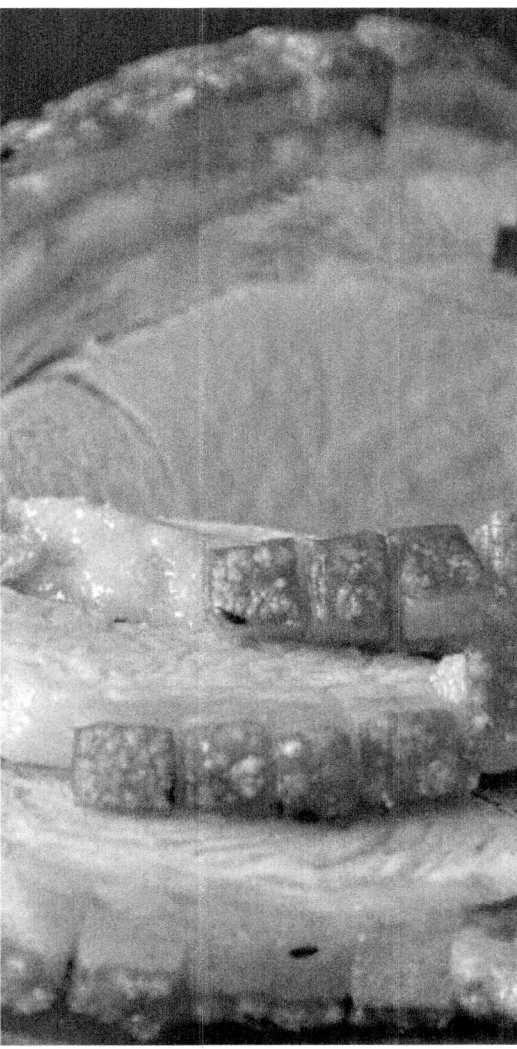

Simple Reduction Smoothie
Prep time: 5 minutes | Cook time: 0 minutes | Serves 2

1 carrot with greens
1 apple, cored and quartered
1 cucumber, quartered
2 kale leaves

1. Blend all ingredients together and enjoy.

PER SERVING
Calories: 85.9 | Fat: 0.9g | Protein: 1.9g | Carbohydrates: 19.9g | Fiber: 4.9g | Sugar: 12.9g | Sodium: 34.9mg

Apple and Orange-Banana Smoothie
Prep time: 10 minutes | Cook time: 0 minutes | Serves 2

1 scoop protein powder
1 cup water
1 apple, cored, seeded, and quartered
1 medium orange, peeled and quartered
1 banana, sliced
2 handfuls spinach
1 medium carrot, peeled and sliced

1. Add liquid first, then softer ingredients and harder items like ice or frozen fruit last.
2. Blend on medium and increase to high for 1 minute.
3. Repeat as necessary.

PER SERVING
Calories: 96.9 | Fat: 0.9g | Protein: 6.9g | Carbohydrates: 14.9g | Fiber: 2.9g | Sugar: 9.9g| Sodium: 35.9mg

Milky Mango with Avocado Smoothie
Prep time: 10 minutes | Cook time: 0 minutes | Serves 2

½ an avocado
½ cup kale
1 tablespoon cacao nibs
½ cup Greek yogurt
½ cup vanilla almond milk
½ cup frozen mango
2 teaspoon honey

1. Add liquid first, then softer ingredients and harder items like ice or frozen fruit last.
2. Blend on medium and increase to high for 1 minute.
3. Repeat as necessary.

PER SERVING

Calories: 70.9| Fat: 0.9g | Protein: 0.9g | Carbohydrates: 15.9g | Fiber: 0.9g | Sugar: 14.9g| Sodium: 39.9mg

Icey Celery with Carrot Smoothie
Prep time: 10 minutes | Cook time: 0 minutes | Serves 1

½ cup apple juice
1 cup tomato juice
1 ½ cups chopped tomatoes
⅔ cups chopped carrots
⅔ cups chopped celery
⅔ teaspoons hot sauce
9 ice cubes

1. Turn your blender on
2. Blend all ingredients on high for 45 seconds, or until desired consistency is reached.

PER SERVING

Calories: 94.9| Fat: 0.9g | Protein: 2.9g | Carbohydrates: 21.9g | Fiber: 3.9g | Sugar: 2.9g| Sodium: 461mg

Fresh Ginger and Strawberry Smoothie

Prep time: 5 minutes | Cook time: 0 minutes | Serves 2

2 cups strongly brewed green tea or jasmine green tea, chilled (see tip)
3 cups fresh or frozen strawberries, hulled and sliced
1 tablespoon grated fresh ginger or 1 teaspoon ground
¼ cup crushed ice (optional)

1. Turn your blender on
2. Blend all ingredients on high for 30-45 seconds, or until desired consistency is reached.
3. Taste Tip: For a stronger green tea flavor, freeze green tea in ice cube trays and use it in place of the crushed ice.

PER SERVING

Calories: 71.9 | Fat: 0.9g | Protein: 1.9g | Carbohydrates: 16.9g | Fiber: 3.9g | Sugar: 10.9g | Sodium: 9.9mg

Homemade Margarita Smoothie

Prep time: 5 minutes | Cook time: 0 minutes | Serves 3 cups

4 celery stalks
2 apples, cored and quartered
2 limes, peeled
1 cup water

1. Pulse the celery first, and then blend in the apples and the limes.
2. Stir gently and enjoy!

PER SERVING

Calories: 73.9 | Fat: 0.2g | Protein: 0.9g | Carbohydrates: 19.9g | Fiber: 3.3g | Sugar: 12.9g | Sodium: 21.9mg

Chapter 7
Detoxifying Smoothies

Lettuce with Minty Apple Smoothie
Prep time: 5 minutes | Cook time: 0 minutes | Serves 2

½ cup mixed berries (frozen or fresh)
10 leaves of mint
1 apple (peeled, sliced and seeds removed)
5 romaine lettuce leaves
20 ounces purified water (use juice if desired)

1. Turn on your blender
2. Blend this delicious smoothie on high for 45 seconds, or until desired consistency is reached.

PER SERVING

Calories: 92.9 | Fat: 0.9g | Protein: 1.9g | Carbohydrates: 21.9g | Fiber: 6.9g | Sugar: 8.9g | Sodium: 17.9mg

Cucumber with Lemony Cilantro Smoothie
Prep time: 10 minutes | Cook time: 0 minutes | Serves 2

½ cucumber (sliced)
1 cup kale (or romaine lettuce or spinach)
1 ½ cups spring water
1/3 cup cilantro (chopped)
½ lemon (peeled and de-seeded)
1 wedge lime (peeled and de-seeded)
½ cup cilantro

1. Turn on your blender
2. Blend all ingredients on high for 30-45 seconds, or until desired consistency is reached.

PER SERVING

Calories: 38.9 | Fat: 0.1g | Protein: 1.9g | Carbohydrates: 9.9g | Fiber: 1.9g | Sugar: 0.9g | Sodium: 19.9mg

Lemon with Sweetened Blueberry Smoothie

Prep time: 10 minutes | Cook time: 0 minutes | Serves 2

½ cup blueberries
2 lemons (peeled, sliced and seeds removed)
2 tablespoons sweetener (honey, or your choice)
2 ½ cups purified water

1. Turn on your blender
2. Blend this deliciously tangy smoothie on high for about 45 seconds, or until desired consistency is reached.

PER SERVING

Calories: 37.9 | Fat: 0g | Protein: 0.9g | Carbohydrates: 12.9g | Fiber: 3.9g | Sugar: 16.9g | Sodium: 0.9mg

Spicy Zucchini Smoothie

Prep time: 10 minutes | Cook time: 0 minutes | Serves 2

1 zucchini
1 tablespoon sea beans
½ lemon, juiced
1 teaspoon maqui berry powder
8 tablespoons grape tomatoes
6 tablespoons celery stocks
½ jalapeno pepper, seeded
1 cup of water
1 cup ice

1. Add all the listed ingredients to blender except zucchini
2. Add zucchini and blend the mixture
3. Blend until smooth
4. Serve chilled and enjoy!

PER SERVING

Calories: 49.9 | Fat: 0.4g | Protein: 2.3g | Carbohydrates: 9.9g | Fiber: 0.9g | Sugar: 5.9g | Sodium: 18.9mg

Gingery Collar Green and Pear Smoothie

Prep time: 10 minutes | Cook time: 0 minutes | Serves 2

3 tablespoons collard greens
1 tablespoon chamomile flowers, dried
1 pear, chopped
1 cantaloupe, sliced and chopped
½ inch ginger, peeled
½ lemon, juiced
1 cup ice
1 cup of water

1. Add all the listed ingredients to a blender
2. Blend until smooth
3. Serve chilled and enjoy!

PER SERVING

Calories: 85.9 | Fat: 0g | Protein: 1.9g | Carbohydrates: 21.9g | Fiber: 4.9g | Sugar: 9.9g | Sodium: 4.9mg

Lemony Cucumber and Iced Apple Smoothie

Prep time: 10 minutes | Cook time: 0 minutes | Serves 2

3 tablespoons collard green
½ teaspoon charcoal activated
1 apple, chopped
1 lemon, peeled
½ inch ginger
1 cucumber, chopped
1 cup ice
1 cup of water

1. Add all the listed ingredients to blender except kiwis
2. Blend until smooth
3. Add kiwis and blend again
4. Serve chilled and enjoy!

PER SERVING

Calories: 87.9 | Fat: 0.9g | Protein: 1.9g | Carbohydrates: 22.9g | Fiber: 0.9g | Sugar: 6.9g | Sodium: 0.9mg

Healthy Beet Smoothie
Prep time: 10 minutes | Cook time: 0 minutes | Serves 2

8 tablespoons beets, chopped
1 lemon, peeled
½ teaspoon wheatgrass
½ inch ginger, peeled
4 tablespoons mango, sliced
1 cup ice
1 cup of water

1. Add all the listed ingredients to a blender
2. Blend until smooth
3. Serve chilled and enjoy!

PER SERVING
Calories: 41.9 | Fat: 0g | Protein: 0.9g | Carbohydrates: 9.9g | Fiber: 0.9g | Sugar: 5.9g | Sodium: 27.9mg

Gingery Cantaloupe Smoothie
Prep time: 10 minutes | Cook time: 0 minutes | Serves 2

1 cantaloupe, sliced
½ inch ginger, peeled
1 tablespoon flaxseed
1 pear, chopped
1 cup of water
1 cup ice

1. Add all the listed ingredients to a blender except the ginger
2. Blend until smooth
3. Then add ginger and blend again
4. Serve chilled and enjoy!

PER SERVING
Calories: 84.9 | Fat: 1.9g | Protein: 1.9g | Carbohydrates: 18.9g | Fiber: 2.9g | Sugar: 6.9g | Sodium: 2.9mg

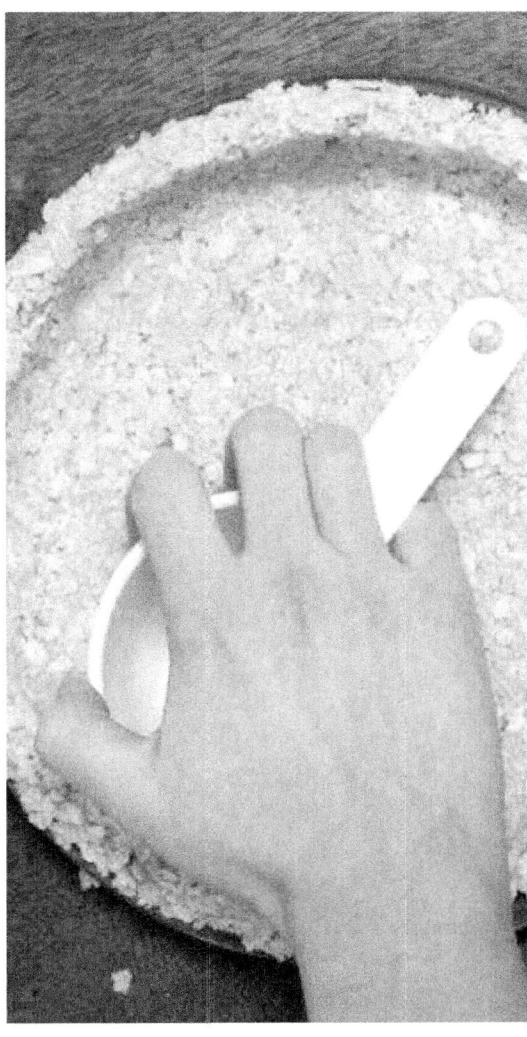

Succulent Banana and Blueberry Smoothie

Prep time: 5 minutes | Cook time: 0 minutes | Serves 1

½ cup frozen blueberries
¼ cup unsweetened cranberry juice
2 bananas

1. Add liquid first, then softer ingredients and harder items like ice or frozen fruit last.
2. Blend on medium and increase to high for 1 minute.
3. Repeat as necessary.

PER SERVING

Calories: 71.9 | Fat: 0.9g | Protein: 7.9g | Carbohydrates: 70.9g | Fiber: 7.9g | Sugar: 14.9g | Sodium: 1.9mg

Superb Ginger Root Smoothie

Prep time: 5 minutes | Cook time: 0 minutes | Serves 1

1 (12-ounce) glass water, at room temperature
½ of lemon juice
½ inch knob of ginger root

1. Add liquid first, then softer ingredients and harder items like ice or frozen fruit last.
2. Blend on medium and later increase for 1 minute. Repeat as necessary.

PER SERVING

Calories: 5.9 | Fat: 0g | Protein: 0g | Carbohydrates: 1.9g | Fiber: 0g | Sugar: 0.9g | Sodium: 6.9mg

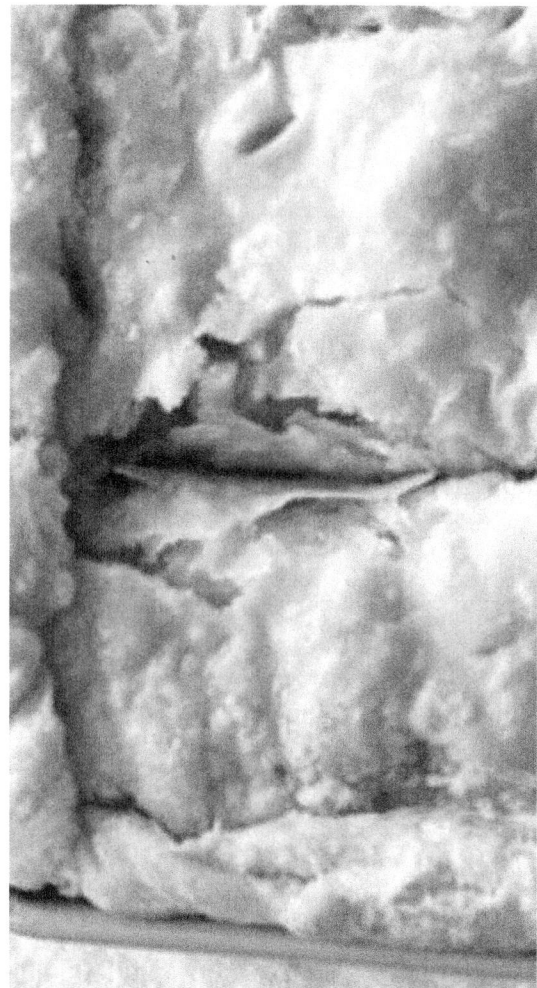

Carroty Clementine Beet Smoothie
Prep time: 10 minutes | Cook time: 0 minutes | Serves 1

1 carrot, peeled, sliced
1 beet, peeled, sliced
½ cup red grapes
1 clementine, peeled
1 slice of ginger, peeled, about the size of a quarter
½ cup green tea

1. Add liquid first, then softer ingredients and harder items like ice or frozen fruit last.
2. Blend on medium and increase to high for 1 minute.
3. Repeat as necessary.

PER SERVING

Calories: 52.9 | Fat: 0g | Protein: 0.9g | Carbohydrates: 14.9g | Fiber: 1.9g | Sugar: 11.9g | Sodium: 34.9mg

Classy Spinach with Blueberry Smoothie
Prep time: 10 minutes | Cook time: 0 minutes | Serves 2

1 cup strawberries
2 cups spinach, raw
½ cup blueberries
½ cup Greek yogurt
2 cups of water

1. Add listed ingredients to a blender
2. Blend until you have a smooth and creamy texture
3. Serve chilled and enjoy!

PER SERVING

Calories: 87.9 | Fat: 1.4g | Protein: 6.9g | Carbohydrates: 13.9g | Fiber: 2.9g | Sugar: 6.9g | Sodium: 24.9mg

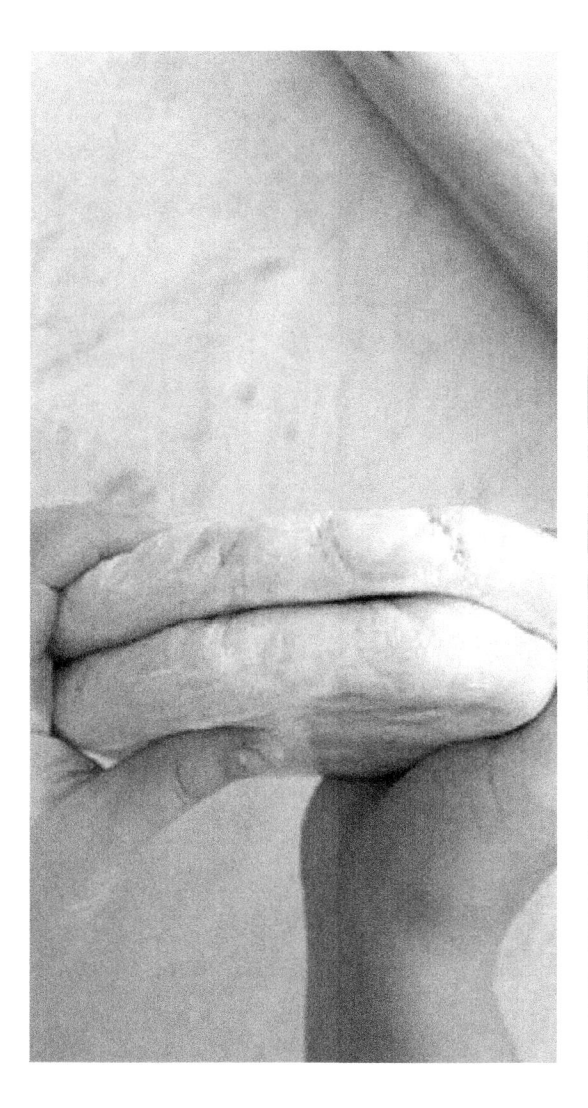

Chilled Zucchini with Tomato Smoothie
Prep time: 10 minutes | Cook time: 0 minutes | Serves 2

1 zucchini
1 tablespoon sea beans
½ lemon, juiced
1 teaspoon maqui berry powder
8 tablespoons grape tomatoes
6 tablespoons celery stocks
½ jalapeno pepper, seeded
1 cup of water
1 cup ice

1. Add all the listed ingredients to blender except zucchini
2. Add zucchini and blend the mixture
3. Blend until smooth
4. Serve chilled and enjoy!

PER SERVING

Calories: 49.9 | Fat: 0g | Protein:2.9g | Carbohydrates: 9.9g | Fiber: 5.9g | Sugar: 18.9g | Sodium: 16.9mg

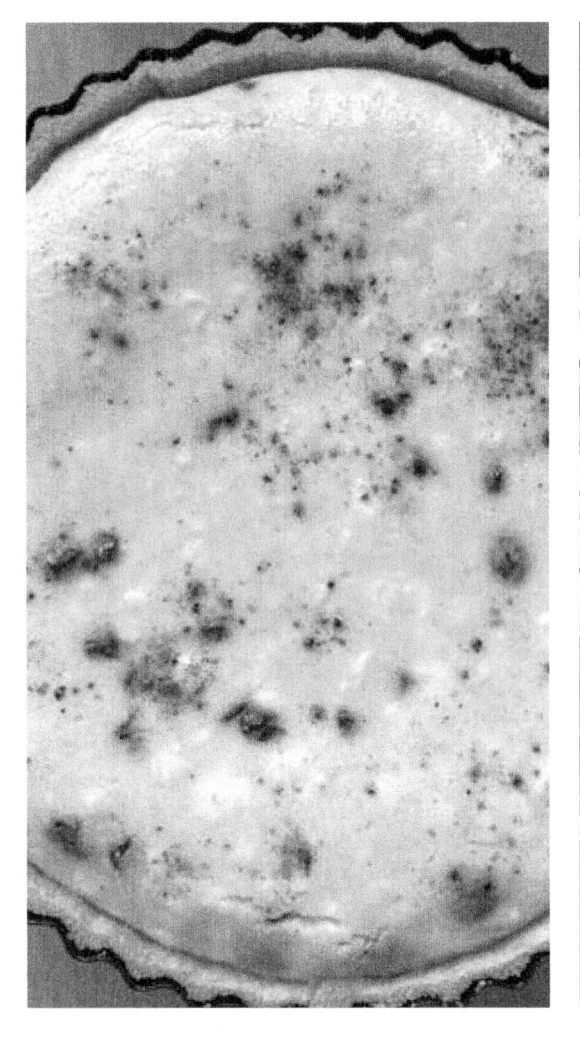

Gingered Cantaloupe and Pear Smoothie
Prep time: 10 minutes | Cook time: 0 minutes | Serves 2

3 tablespoons collard greens
1 tablespoon chamomile flowers, dried
1 pear, chopped
1 cantaloupe, sliced and chopped
½ inch ginger, peeled
½ lemon, juiced
1 cup ice
1 cup of water

1. Add all the listed ingredients to a blender
2. Blend until smooth
3. Serve chilled and enjoy!

PER SERVING

Calories: 56.9 | Fat: 0g | Protein:0g | Carbohydrates: 14.9g | Fiber: 2.9g | Sugar: 9.9g | Sodium: 4.9mg

Chilled Detoxification Smoothie
Prep time: 5 minutes | Cook time: 0 minutes | Serves 1

25 ounces cold water
2 tablespoon apple cider vinegar
1 full lemon
Ice

OPTIONAL:

Cinnamon
Stevia

1. Add liquid first, then softer ingredients and harder items like ice or frozen fruit last.
2. Blend on medium and increase to high for 1 minute.
3. Repeat as necessary.

PER SERVING

Calories: 16.9| Fat: 0g | Protein: 0g | Carbohydrates: 0g | Fiber: 3.9g | Sugar: 10.9g| Sodium: 15.9mg

Minty Lettuce and Apple Smoothie
Prep time: 10 minutes | Cook time: 0 minutes | Serves 2

½ cup mixed berries (frozen or fresh)
10 leaves of mint
1 apple (peeled, sliced and seeds removed)
5 romaine lettuce leaves
20 ounces purified water (use juice if desired)

1. Turn your blender on
2. Blend this delicious smoothie on high for 45 seconds, or until desired consistency is reached.

PER SERVING

Calories: 92.9| Fat: 0.9g | Protein: 1.9g | Carbohydrates: 21.9g | Fiber: 6.9g | Sugar: 4.9g| Sodium: 17.9mg

Lemony Cucumber and Charcoal Smoothie

Prep time: 10 minutes | Cook time: 0 minutes | Serves 2

3 tablespoons collard green
½ teaspoon charcoal activated
1 apple, chopped
1 lemon, peeled
½ inch ginger
1 cucumber, chopped
1 cup ice
1 cup of water

1. Add all the listed ingredients to blender except kiwis
2. Blend until smooth
3. Add kiwis and blend again
4. Serve chilled and enjoy!

PER SERVING

Calories: 87.9 | Fat: 0.9g | Protein: 1.9g | Carbohydrates: 22.9g | Fiber: 2.9g | Sugar: 10.9g | Sodium: 5.9mg

Limy Cilantro Smoothie

Prep time: 10 minutes | Cook time: 0 minutes | Serves 2

½ cucumber (sliced)
1 cup kale (or romaine lettuce or spinach)
1 ½ cups spring water
⅓ cup cilantro (chopped)
½ lemon (peeled and de-seeded)
1 wedge lime (peeled and de-seeded)
½ cup cilantro

1. Turn your blender on
2. Blend all ingredients on high for 30 -45 seconds, or until desired consistency is reached.

PER SERVING

Calories: 38.9| Fat: 0g | Protein: 1.9g | Carbohydrates: 9.9g | Fiber: 1.9g | Sugar: 1.9g| Sodium: 19.9mg

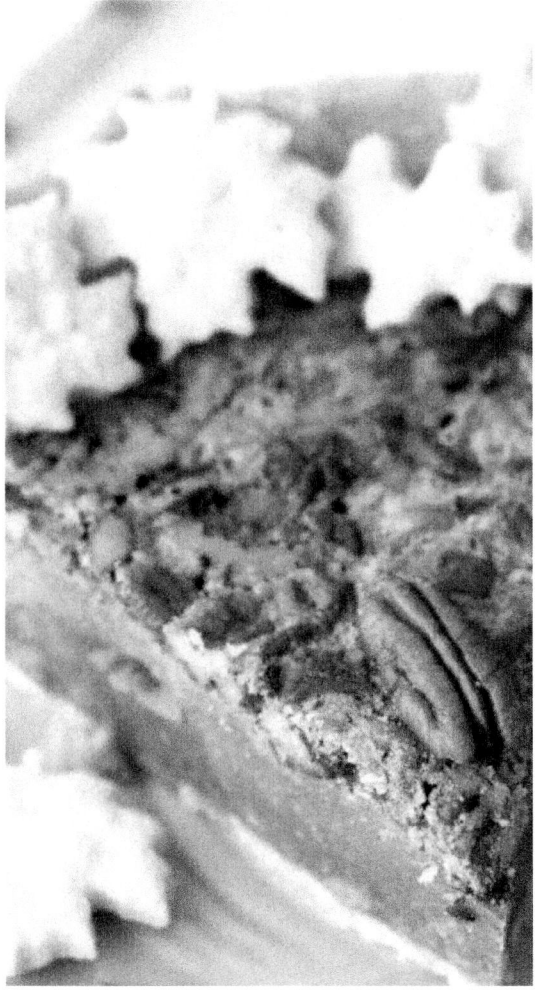

Tangy Blueberry Smoothie

Prep time: 5 minutes | Cook time: 0 minutes | Serves 2

½ cup blueberries
2 lemons (peeled, sliced and seeds removed)
2 tablespoons sweetener (honey, or your choice)
2 ½ cups purified water

1. Turn your blender on.
2. Blend this deliciously tangy smoothie on high for about 45 seconds, or until desired consistency is reached.

PER SERVING
Calories: 37.9| Fat: 0g | Protein: 0.9g | Carbohydrates: 12.9g | Fiber: 3.9g | Sugar: 20.9g| Sodium: 0.9mg

Chapter 8
Energy Boosting Smoothies

Limy Blackberry and Date Smoothie

Prep time: 5 minutes | Cook time: 0 minutes | Serves 2

1½ cups water
2 cups frozen blackberries
1 lime, zested, peeled, and quartered
2 dates, pitted

1. Turn your blender on
2. Blend all ingredients on high for 30-45 seconds, or until desired consistency is reached.
3. Tip: Add a few mint leaves for their digestive benefits and flavor.

PER SERVING

Calories: 94.9 | Fat: 0.9g | Protein: 1.9g | Carbohydrates: 23.9g | Fiber: 8.9g | Sugar: 12.9g | Sodium: 1.9mg

Milky Berry and Cardamom Smoothie

Prep time: 5 minutes | Cook time: 0 minutes | Serves 2

1½ cups water or nondairy or dairy milk of choice
1 cup frozen blueberries
1 cup frozen blackberries
1 teaspoon vanilla extract
⅛ teaspoon ground cardamom

1. Turn your blender on
2. Blend all ingredients on high for 30-45 seconds, or until desired consistency is reached.
3. Substitute It! If you are unable to locate ground cardamom, try 1 teaspoon fresh ginger or 1 teaspoon ground cinnamon.

PER SERVING

Calories: 78.9 | Fat: 0.9g | Protein: 1.9g | Carbohydrates: 17.9g | Fiber: 5.9g | Sugar: 10.9g | Sodium: 1.9mg

Simple Nut-Milk Smoothie
Prep time: 5 minutes | Cook time: 0 minutes | Serves 2-4

1 cup nuts or seeds (or a mix of both), soaked for 2 to 6 hours
2 to 4 cups water
Pinch salt
Sweetener of choice (optional)

1. Turn your blender on
2. Blend all ingredients on high for 30-45 seconds, or until desired consistency is reached.
3. Prep Tip: Don't forget to save your nut milk pulp for use in baking or dry it out and use it as breadcrumbs.

PER SERVING

Calories: 39.9 | Fat: 2.9g | Protein: 0.9g | Carbohydrates: 5.9g | Fiber: 0g | Sugar: 0.9g | Sodium: 99mg

Lemony Banana-Pear Smoothie
Prep time: 5 minutes | Cook time: 0 minutes | Serves 2

1½ cups water or nondairy or dairy milk of choice
½ cup arugula, lightly packed
½ cup watercress, lightly packed
½ cup spinach, lightly packed
1 pear, cut into 1-inch chunks
1 frozen banana
1 tablespoon freshly squeezed lemon juice

1. Turn your blender on
2. Blend all ingredients on high for 30-45 seconds, or until desired consistency is reached.

PER SERVING

Calories: 98.9 | Fat: 0.9g | Protein: 1.9g | Carbohydrates: 24.9g | Fiber: 3.9g | Sugar: 13.9g | Sodium: 15.9mg

Gingered Pineapple and Turmeric Energizer
Prep time: 5 minutes | Cook time: 0 minutes | Serves 2

1½ cups water or nondairy or dairy milk of choice
2 cups spinach, lightly packed (see tip)
2 cups frozen pineapple chunks
1 tablespoon freshly squeezed lemon juice
1 teaspoon ground turmeric
1 teaspoon grated fresh ginger or ½ teaspoon ground

1. Turn your blender on
2. Blend all ingredients on high for 30-45 seconds, or until desired consistency is reached.
3. Substitute It! Swapping the spinach for kale, chard, or collards will create a more bitter flavor.

PER SERVING

Calories: 95.9 | Fat: 0.9g | Protein: 1.9g | Carbohydrates: 23.9g | Fiber: 2.9g | Sugar: 15.9g | Sodium: 29.9mg

Cucumber with Celery Smoothie
Prep time: 10 minutes | Cook time: 0 minutes | Serves 2

1 cup of kale or spinach (chopped)
1 stalk of celery (chopped)
1 apple (sliced)
1 tablespoon lemon juice
1/3 cucumber (sliced)
1 cup ice cubes
¼ cup spring water

1. Turn your blender on
2. Blend all ingredients on high for 30 -45 seconds, or until desired consistency is reached.

PER SERVING

Calories: 61.9| Fat: 0.2g | Protein: 0.9g | Carbohydrates: 14.9g | Fiber: 2.9g | Sugar: 9.9g | Sodium: 25.9mg

Revitalizing Banana Smoothie
Prep time: 5 minutes | Cook time: 0 minutes | Serves 2

1 banana
1 teaspoon ginger (sliced)
1 cup Swiss chard
½ cup blueberries
1 cup spring water or coconut water
½ cup ice

1. Turn on your blender
2. Blend all ingredients on high for 30 -45 seconds, or until desired consistency is reached.

PER SERVING

Calories: 79.9 | Fat: 0.3g | Protein: 1.2g | Carbohydrates: 19.9g | Fiber: 2.9g | Sugar: 10.9g | Sodium: 40.9mg

Energizing Banana-Kiwi Smoothie
Prep time: 10 minutes | Cook time: 0 minutes | Serves 4

2 cups (500 ml) mâché salad (also called lamb's lettuce, valerian, corn salad)
2 kiwis
1 ½ banana, frozen
1 cup pineapple (250 ml)
1 cup green tea, cold (250 ml)

1. Add liquid first, then softer ingredients and harder items like ice or frozen fruit last.
2. Blend on medium and increase to high for 1 minute.
3. Repeat as necessary.

PER SERVING

Calories: 81.9| Fat: 0g | Protein: 0.9g | Carbohydrates: 20.9g | Fiber: 1.9g | Sugar: 14.9g| Sodium: 5.9mg

Homemade Celery and Apple Smoothie

Prep time: 10 minutes | Cook time: 0 minutes | Serves 2

1 cup of kale or spinach (chopped)
1 stalk of celery (chopped)
1 apple (sliced)
1 tablespoon lemon juice
⅓ cucumber (sliced)
1 cup ice cubes
¼ cup spring water

1. Turn on your blender
2. Blend all ingredients on high for 30 to 45 seconds, or until desired consistency is reached.

PER SERVING
Calories: 61.9 | Fat: 0g | Protein: 0.9g | Carbohydrates: 14.9g | Fiber: 2.9g | Sugar: 15.9g | Sodium: 25.9mg

Chapter 9
Anti-Aging Smoothies

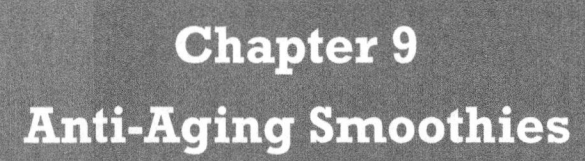

Refreshing Veggie Smoothie

Prep time: 5 minutes | Cook time: 0 minutes | Serves 2

1 medium tomato
½ red bell pepper
2 cloves garlic
1 celery stalk
1 carrot (sliced)
1 cup kale (or romaine lettuce)
1 cup ice cubes

1. Turn on your blender
2. Blend all ingredients on high for 30 -45 seconds, or until desired consistency is reached.

PER SERVING

Calories: 54.9 | Fat: 0.1g | Protein: 1.9g | Carbohydrates: 11.9g | Fiber: 2.9g | Sugar: 3.9g | Sodium: 50.9mg

Classy Avocado Smoothie

Prep time: 10 minutes | Cook time: 0 minutes | Serves 2

½ avocado (ripe) or 4 tablespoons almond butter
½ cucumber
1 cup kale or Bok Choy or romaine lettuce
½ banana
¾ cups blueberries
1 cup spring water or coconut water

1. We don't recommend a sweetener for this, but if you must, go lightly and use honey if necessary.
2. Turn on your blender
3. Blend all ingredients on high, or until desired consistency is reached.

PER SERVING

Calories: 89.9 | Fat: 0.9g | Protein: 1.9g | Carbohydrates: 20.9g | Fiber: 2.9g | Sugar: 9.9g | Sodium: 16.9mg

Tropical Pineapple Smoothie

Prep time: 10 minutes | Cook time: 0 minutes | Serves 1

1 cup coconut water
1 tablespoon chia seeds
1 cup pineapple, sliced
½ cup mango, sliced

1. Add all the listed ingredients to a blender
2. Blend until you have a smooth and creamy texture
3. Serve chilled and enjoy!

PER SERVING

Calories: 89.9 | Fat: 4.9g | Protein: 3.9g | Carbohydrates: 10.9g | Fiber: 2.9g | Sugar: 14.9g | Sodium: 126mg

Soothing Strawberry and Cucumber Smoothie

Prep time: 5 minutes | Cook time: 0 minutes | Serves 2 cups

6 strawberries, capped
1 banana, peeled
1 pomegranate seed
1 cucumber, quartered

1. Add all the ingredients to your blender, and puree. You'll get the benefit from the fiber and the nutrients in the skins as well!
2. If needed, add a little water for a drinkable consistency.

PER SERVING

Calories: 75.9 | Fat: 0.4g | Protein: 1.4g | Carbohydrates: 17.9g | Fiber: 2.9g | Sugar: 9.9g | Sodium: 2.9mg

Simple Berry Smoothie
Prep time: 5 minutes | Cook time: 0 minutes | Serves 3 cups

6 medium strawberries, capped
¼ honeydew, peeled and seeded
½ cup blueberries
1 cucumber, quartered

1. Simply blend together.
2. The cucumber does an excellent job of cutting down some of the sweet flavor and lightening up the smoothie.

PER SERVING

Calories: 53.9 | Fat: 0.2g | Protein: 0.9g | Carbohydrates: 12.9g | Fiber: 1.9g | Sugar: 10.9g | Sodium: 2.9mg

Easy Watermelon with Plum Smoothie
Prep time: 5 minutes | Cook time: 0 minutes | Serves 2 cups

2 plums
1 cup watermelon
1 small cucumber, quartered

1. Blend the ingredients and drink immediately.
2. There should be exactly enough for 1 serving. Just delicious!

PER SERVING

Calories: 45.9| Fat: 0.2g | Protein: 0.9g | Carbohydrates: 9.9g | Fiber: 0.9g | Sugar: 7.9g | Sodium: 1.9mg

Anti-aging Veggie Boost
Prep time: 5 minutes | Cook time: 0 minutes | Serves 2 cups

½ cup water
2 cups spinach
3 basil leaves
6 Brussels sprouts
¼ fennel bulb
1 cucumber, quartered

1. Blend the water, spinach, basil, and Brussels sprouts, pulsing until they're in small chunks.
2. Next, blend the fennel and the cucumber.
3. If you'd like, add some black pepper, a pinch of sea salt, or maybe even a jalapeño.

PER SERVING

Calories: 52.9 | Fat: 0.4g | Protein: 3.9g | Carbohydrates: 9.9g | Fiber: 3.9g | Sugar: 2.9g | Sodium: 55.9mg

Best Hangover Smoothie
Prep time: 5 minutes | Cook time: 0 minutes | Serves 2 cups

1 cup cauliflower
1 cup broccoli florets
1 apple, cored and quartered
1 orange, peeled

1. Blend the vegetables first, then the fruits.
2. Drink on your way to work, and you'll be feeling better within the hour!
3. If your hangover persists, drink another glass.

PER SERVING

Calories: 51.9 | Fat: 0.3g | Protein: 2.2g | Carbohydrates: 11.9g | Fiber: 2.9g | Sugar: 6.9g | Sodium: 22.9mg

Carroty Beet Smoothie

Prep time: 5 minutes | Cook time: 0 minutes | Serves 2 cups

1 yellow beet
1 carrot with greens
1 orange, peeled
½ cup coconut water

1. Pulse the beet and the carrot, then add the orange and coconut water.

PER SERVING

Calories: 37.9| Fat: 0.1g | Protein: 0.9g | Carbohydrates: 7.9g | Fiber: 2.9g | Sugar: 4.9g | Sodium: 163mg

Lemony Cranberry Smoothie

Prep time: 5 minutes | Cook time: 0 minutes | Serves 4 cups

1 cup cranberries
2 lemons, peeled
3 cups water

1. Light and refreshing, this smoothie is made by simply blending the cranberries and lemons, then adding the water.
2. The lemons prevent oxidation, so go ahead and make multiple servings, even if you won't be drinking them right away—they won't lose their nutritional value. Enjoy!

PER SERVING

Calories: 38.9 | Fat: 0.02g | Protein: 0.0g | Carbohydrates: 9.9g | Fiber: 0.0g | Sugar: 7.9g | Sodium: 4.9mg

Restorative Broccoli Smoothie
Prep time: 10 minutes | Cook time: 0 minutes | Serves 3 cups

1 cup broccoli florets
2 stalks celery
2 cups spinach
1 clove garlic, peeled
¼ head cabbage
1 cup water

1. Blend all ingredients together.

PER SERVING

Calories: 24.9 | Fat: 0.14g | Protein: 1.9g | Carbohydrates: 4.9g | Fiber: 1.9g | Sugar: 1.9g | Sodium: 43.9mg

Refreshing Potato Smoothie
Prep time: 5 minutes | Cook time: 0 minutes | Serves 3 cups

1 small, sweet potato
1 small white potato
¼ cantaloupe, peeled and seeded
¼ cucumber, quartered

1. Chop the sweet potato and white potato into 1-inch cubes.
2. Pulse the potatoes, then add the rest of the ingredients.
3. This one's refreshing as well as good for your skin.

PER SERVING

Calories: 41.9 | Fat: 0.0g | Protein: 0.9g | Carbohydrates: 8.9g | Fiber: 1.4g | Sugar: 1.9g | Sodium: 12.9mg

Spiced Veggie Smoothie

Prep time: 5 minutes | Cook time: 0 minutes | Serves 3 cups

1 cup broccoli florets
1 carrot with greens
2 cups spinach
6 Brussels sprouts
1 cup water

1. Pulse all vegetables first, then add water and blend.
2. For a snappy kick, try adding some jalapeño pepper.

PER SERVING

Calories: 31.9 | Fat: 0.2g | Protein: 2.4g | Carbohydrates: 5.9g | Fiber: 2.9g | Sugar: 1.9g | Sodium: 44.9mg

Delectable Kale and Cucumber Smoothie

Prep time: 10 minutes | Cook time: 0 minutes | Serves 3 cups

2 kale leaves
1 cup spinach
1 lime, peeled
1 green bell pepper, de-stemmed
1 cucumber, quartered
1 carrot with greens

1. Pulse the kale, spinach, and lime.
2. Add the pepper, cucumber, and carrot.
3. You may want to add ½ cup water to the smoothie to loosen it up a bit.

PER SERVING

Calories: 37.9 | Fat: 0.3g | Protein: 1.9g | Carbohydrates: 7.9g | Fiber: 1.9g | Sugar: 2.9g | Sodium: 31.9mg

Minty Plum Smoothie

Prep time: 5 minutes | Cook time: 0 minutes | Serves 2 cups

½ cup water
1 plum, pitted
2 kiwis, peeled
2 cups spinach
6 mint leaves, plus 1 for garnish
1 teaspoon ginger, grated

1. Add the water, plum, and kiwis to your blender, and pulse for a few seconds. Add the spinach, mint, ginger, and puree.
2. Garnish with a mint leaf and enjoy!

PER SERVING

Calories: 50.9 | Fat: 0.2g | Protein: 1.9g | Carbohydrates: 11.9g | Fiber: 1.9g | Sugar: 7.9g | Sodium: 31.9mg

Classical Italiana Smoothie

Prep time: 5 minutes | Cook time: 0 minutes | Serves 2 cups

1 tomato
1 clove garlic
1 green bell pepper, de-stemmed
3 basil leaves
2 kale leaves

1. If this smoothie is a bit too thick, just add water. It can work equally well for lunch or dinner.
2. As a matter of fact, if you'd like to leave it a bit thick, it's great as a chilled soup.

PER SERVING

Calories: 22.9 | Fat: 0.1g | Protein: 0.9g | Carbohydrates: 4.9g | Fiber: 0.9g | Sugar: 1.9g | Sodium: 4.9mg

Coconutty Parsley and Apple Smoothie

Prep time: 10 minutes | Cook time: 0 minutes | Serves 2

1 ½ cup kale cut up
2 Celery sticks
1 whole lemon juice
1 medium apple (Cored)
1 handful parsley
1 ½ cup coconut water

1. Add liquid first, then softer ingredients and harder items like ice or frozen fruit last.
2. Blend on medium and increase to high for 1 minute.
3. Repeat as necessary.

PER SERVING

Calories: 95.9 | Fat: 0.9g | Protein: 1.9g | Carbohydrates: 21.9g | Fiber: 4.9g | Sugar: 14.9g| Sodium: 208mg

Best Mango and Pineapple Smoothie

Prep time: 5 minutes | Cook time: 0 minutes | Serves 1

1 cup coconut water
1 tablespoon chia seeds
1 cup pineapple, sliced
½ cup mango, sliced

1. Add all the listed ingredients to a blender
2. Blend until you have a smooth and creamy texture
3. Serve chilled and enjoy!

PER SERVING

Calories: 89.9| Fat: 4.9g | Protein: 3.9g | Carbohydrates: 10.9g | Fiber: 5.9g | Sugar: 14.9g| Sodium: 254mg

Chapter 10
Dessert Smoothies

Milk with Chocolaty Frappé
Prep time: 5 minutes | Cook time: 0 minutes | Serves 2

1 cup strong brewed coffee, cooled
½ cup reduced-fat (2%) milk
2 tablespoons sugar
1 tablespoon light chocolate syrup
Ice cubes

1. Combine the ingredients in a blender and blend until smooth.
2. Pour into two glasses and serve immediately.
3. Variation: Substitute ½ teaspoon vanilla, almond extract or ground cinnamon for the chocolate syrup.

PER SERVING

Calories: 89.9| Fat: 1.4g | Protein: 1.9g | Carbohydrates: 18.9g | Fiber: 0g | Sugar: 12.9g | Sodium: 39.9mg

Sugary Green Tea Smoothie
Prep time: 5 minutes | Cook time: 0 minutes | Serves 2

1 cup boiling water
4 green tea with mandarin orange flavor tea bags
2 teaspoons sugar
1 medium ripe banana
½ cup ice cubes (about 3 to 4)

1. Pour the boiling water over the tea bags, cover, and brew for 1 ½ minutes. Remove the tea bags and squeeze.
2. Stir in the sugar and chill.
3. In a blender, process the tea, banana, and ice cubes until blended.

PER SERVING

Calories: 79.9 | Fat: 0g | Protein: 0.9g | Carbohydrates: 18.9g | Fiber: 1.9g | Sugar: 8.9g | Sodium: 4.9mg

Limy Mango Smoothie
Prep time: 10 minutes | Cook time: 0 minutes | Serves 4

2 cups frozen mango cubes
2 containers (6-ounces, each) vanilla low-fat yogurt
¾ cup orange juice
½ lime juice
1 teaspoon vanilla (optional)
1/8 teaspoon salt

1. Place all the ingredients in a blender or food processor and blend on medium speed until smooth.
2. Serve immediately in dessert, wine, or champagne glasses.
3. Ingredients Tip: You can find frozen mango cubes in the supermarket near the other frozen fruit. If you can't find frozen mango cubes, you can make your own. Cut the mango into 1-inch chunks, place them on a cookie sheet and freeze for about 3 hours.

PER SERVING
Calories: 92.9 | Fat: 0.4g | Protein: 2.9g | Carbohydrates: 20.9g | Fiber: 0.9g | Sugar: 26.9g | Sodium: 38.9mg

Tasty Banana Shake
Prep time: 5 minutes | Cook time: 0 minutes | Serves 2

½ banana
½ cup sliced strawberries, hulls removed
½ cup low-sugar orange juice drink
¼ avocado, peel and pit removed
Ice

1. Peel the banana, cut into slices and place in a blender.
2. Add the remaining ingredients to the blender and blend until smooth.
3. Pour into serving glasses.

PER SERVING
Calories: 89.9 | Fat: 2.4g | Protein: 0.9g | Carbohydrates: 17.9g | Fiber: 2.9g | Sugar: 8.9g | Sodium: 2.9mg

Perfect Winter Smoothie

Prep time: 5 minutes | Cook time: 0 minutes | Serves 2

½ cup canned yams in light syrup, drained
½ cup apple cider
1 teaspoon sugar-free maple syrup
¼ teaspoon ground cinnamon
Ice
2 cinnamon sticks (optional)

1. Combine all the ingredients except the cinnamon sticks in a blender and blend until smooth.
2. Pour into two glasses and garnish with the cinnamon sticks.

PER SERVING

Calories: 89.9 | Fat: 0g | Protein: 0.9g | Carbohydrates: 19.9g | Fiber: 1.9g | Sugar: 5.9g | Sodium: 24.9mg

Best Beet and Berry Smoothie

Prep time: 5 minutes | Cook time: 0 minutes | Serves 2

½ cup canned sliced beets, drained
½ cup frozen mixed berries
½ cup no-sugar-added orange juice
1 tablespoon lemon juice
1 tablespoon honey
Ice

1. Combine all the ingredients in a blender and blend until smooth.
2. Pour into two glasses.

PER SERVING

Calories: 89.9 | Fat: 0g | Protein: 0.9g | Carbohydrates: 22.9g | Fiber: 1.9g | Sugar: 15.9g | Sodium: 84.9mg

Awesome Spa Smoothie

Prep time: 10 minutes | Cook time: 0 minutes | Serves 2

½ cucumber
½ cup sliced cantaloupe
½ cup fresh sliced strawberries
¼ cup plain non-fat Greek yogurt
1 tablespoon sugar
1 teaspoon grated lemon peel
Ice

1. Peel the cucumber and cut in half. Seed the cucumber, cut into half-moon-shaped slices and place in a blender.
2. Add the cantaloupe, strawberries, yogurt, sugar, lemon peel, and ice to the blender and blend until smooth.
3. Pour into serving glasses.

PER SERVING

Calories: 79.9 | Fat: 0g | Protein: 3.9g | Carbohydrates: 15.9g | Fiber: 1.9g | Sugar: 8.9g | Sodium: 19.9mg

Sweet Cucumber and Berry Smoothie
Prep time: 5 minutes | Cook time: 0 minutes | Serves 1

½ cucumber
½ cup frozen mixed berries
2 teaspoons sugar
Juice and grated peel of ½ lime
Ice

1. Peel the cucumber and cut in half. Seed the cucumber, cut into half-moon-shaped slices and place in a blender.
2. Add the remaining ingredients to the blender and blend until smooth.
3. For smoother consistency, add water as needed, ½ cup at a time.
4. Pour into a serving glass.

PER SERVING
Calories: 89.9 | Fat: 0g | Protein: 0.9g | Carbohydrates: 22.9g | Fiber: 3.9g | Sugar: 12.9g | Sodium: 0mg

Milky Strawberry Pops
Prep time: 10 minutes | Cook time: 0 minutes | Serves 4 pops

1 cup frozen strawberries
1 cup fat-free (skim) milk
½ cup plain non-fat yogurt
1 tablespoon sugar
1 tablespoon lemon juice
4 (5-ounces) paper or plastic cups or pop molds
4 pop sticks

1. Combine the strawberries, milk, yogurt, sugar and lemon juice in a blender or food processor and blend until smooth.
2. Pour the mixture into cups, cover the top of each cup with a small piece of foil, and freeze for 2 hours.
3. Insert the sticks through the center of the foil and freeze for 6 hours or until firm.
4. To serve, remove the foil and peel away the paper cups or gently twist the frozen pops out of the plastic cups.

PER SERVING
Calories: 59.9 | Fat: 0g | Protein: 3.9g | Carbohydrates: 11.9g | Fiber: 0.9g | Sugar: 7.9g | Sodium: 54.9mg

Sweet Basil and Greek Yogurt Pops
Prep time: 10 minutes | Cook time: 0 minutes | Serves 16 pops

1 ¼ cups plain non-fat Greek yogurt
¼ cup milk
Juice and grated peel of 1 lemon
2 tablespoons sugar
2 tablespoons chopped fresh basil
Ice cube trays
Pop sticks

1. Combine the yogurt, milk, lemon juice and peel, sugar and basil in a blender or food processor and blend until smooth.
2. Pour the mixture into the ice cube trays and freeze for 2 hours.
3. Insert sticks and freeze for 4 to 6 hours or until firm.
4. To remove the pops from the trays, place the bottoms of the ice cube trays under warm running water until loosened and press firmly on the bottoms to release. (Do not twist or pull the sticks.)

PER SERVING
Calories: 19.9 | Fat: 0g | Protein: 1.9g | Carbohydrates: 2.9g | Fiber: 0g | Sugar: 0.9g | Sodium: 9.9mg

Chilled Jungle Pops

Prep time: 5 minutes | Cook time: 0 minutes | Serves 4 pops

1 cup frozen strawberries
1 banana, broken into pieces
¾ cup water
½ cup unsweetened plain almond milk
4 (5-ounce) paper or plastic cups
4 pop sticks

1. Combine the strawberries, banana, water and almond milk in a blender or food processor and blend until smooth.
2. Pour the mixture into the cups, cover the top of each cup with a small piece of foil and freeze for 1 hour.
3. Insert the sticks through the center of the foil and freeze for 6 hours or until firm.
4. To serve, remove the foil and peel away the paper cups or gently twist the frozen pops out of the plastic cups.

PER SERVING
Calories: 44.9 | Fat: 0g | Protein: 0.9g | Carbohydrates: 10.9g | Fiber: 1.9g | Sugar: 6.9g | Sodium: 19.9mg

Milky Kiwi and Strawberry Pops
Prep time: 10 minutes | Cook time: 0 minutes | Serves 4 pops

2 kiwis, peeled and sliced
1 container (6-ounces) strawberry-flavor low-fat yogurt
¾ cup fat-free (skim) milk
½ cup frozen strawberries
4 (5-ounce) paper or plastic cups
4 pop sticks

1. Combine the kiwi, yogurt, milk and strawberries in a blender or food processor and blend until smooth.
2. Pour the mixture into the cups, cover the top of each cup with a small piece of foil and freeze for 2 hours.
3. Insert the sticks through the center of the foil and freeze for 6 hours or until firm.
4. To serve, remove the foil and peel away the paper cups or gently twist the frozen pops out of the plastic cups.

PER SERVING

Calories: 89.9 | Fat: 0.4g | Protein: 2.9g | Carbohydrates: 16.9g | Fiber: 0.9g | Sugar: 5.9g | Sodium: 39.9mg

Delicious Yogurt Smoothie
Prep time: 10 minutes | Cook time: 0 minutes | Serves 8 pops

2 cups ice
1 ½ cups vanilla low-fat yogurt
¾ cup frozen orange juice concentrate
½ cup fat-free (skim) milk
¼ teaspoon vanilla
Pop molds with lids
Pop sticks

1. Combine the ice, yogurt, juice concentrate, milk and vanilla in a blender or food processor and blend until smooth.
2. Pour the mixture into the molds, cover it
3. Insert the sticks through the center of the foil and freeze for 6 hours or until firm.
4. To remove the pops from the molds, place the bottom of the pops under warm running water until loosened, then press firmly on the bottoms to release. (Do not twist or pull the lids.)
5. Tip: Frozen juice concentrate works great for frozen pops. Try any desired juice flavor and pair it with yogurt for a creamy fruity treat.

PER SERVING

Calories: 89.9 | Fat: 0.4g | Protein: 2.9g | Carbohydrates: 16.9g | Fiber: 0g | Sugar: 5.9g | Sodium: 34.9mg

Rich Raspberry Cup

Prep time: 10 minutes | Cook time: 0 minutes | Serves 4 pops

1 ¼ cups plain non-fat Greek yogurt, divided
¼ cup milk
2 tablespoons sugar divided
6 teaspoons lemon juice, divided
1 cup chopped raspberries, divided
4 (5-ounce) paper or plastic cups or pop molds.
4 pop sticks

1. Combine ¾ cup yogurt, milk, 1 tablespoon sugar and 3 teaspoons lemon juice in a blender or food processor and blend until smooth, then gently stir in ¼ cup of raspberries.
2. Pour the mixture into the cups and freeze for 1 hour.
3. Combine ½ up raspberries and 1-½ teaspoons lemon juice in a blender or food processor and blend until smooth.
4. Pour the mixture into the cups over the yogurt layer and freeze for 1 hour.
5. Combine the remaining ½ cup of yogurt, ¼ cup raspberries, 1 tablespoon sugar and 1-½ teaspoons lemon juice in a blender or food processor and blend until smooth.
6. Pour the mixture into the cups over the raspberry layer.
7. Cover the top of each cup with a small piece of foil and insert the sticks through the center of the foil, then freeze for 4 hours or until firm.
8. When ready, serve and enjoy!

PER SERVING

Calories: 79.9 | Fat: 0g | Protein: 6.9g | Carbohydrates: 13.9g | Fiber: 1.9g | Sugar: 6.9g | Sodium: 34.9mg

Homemade Purpilicious Pops

Prep time: 10 minutes | Cook time: 0 minutes | Serves 4 pops

1 cup frozen blueberries
¾ cup diet blueberry-pomegranate juice
½ cup raspberry sherbet
½ cup fat-free (skim) milk
2 tablespoons honey
Pop molds or paper or plastic cups
Pop sticks

1. Combine the blueberries, juice, sherbet, milk and honey in a blender or food processor and blend until smooth.
2. Pour the mixture into the molds, cover the top of each mold with a small piece of foil and freeze for 2 hours.
3. Insert the sticks through the center of the foil and freeze for 6 hours or until firm.
4. To remove the pops from the molds, remove the foil and place the bottoms of the pops under warm running water until loosened, then press firmly on the bottoms to release. (Do not twist or pull the sticks).

PER SERVING
Calories: 89.9 | Fat: 0.4g | Protein: 1.9g | Carbohydrates: 20.9g | Fiber: 0.9g | Sugar: 6.9g | Sodium: 29.9mg

Limy Cherry Smoothie

Prep time: 10 minutes | Cook time: 0 minutes | Serves 2

1 cup frozen pitted cherries
1 lime, peeled
½ cup fresh spinach
½ cup chopped cucumber
1½ cups coconut water

1. Put the cherries, lime, spinach, cucumber, and coconut water in a blender.
2. Blend on high speed until smooth.
3. Divide evenly between 2 cups and enjoy!

PER SERVING

Calories: 85.9| Fat: 0.9g | Protein: 2.9g | Carbohydrates: 19.9g | Fiber: 4.2g | Sugar: 11.9g| Sodium: 208mg

Homemade Honey and Turmeric Latte

Prep time: 5 minutes | Cook time: 0 minutes | Serves 2

12 ounces unsweetened vanilla almond milk
1 teaspoon turmeric
½ teaspoon ground ginger
¼ teaspoon cinnamon
1 teaspoon raw honey

1. In a small saucepan, bring the vanilla almond milk to a boil.
2. Remove from heat and add the turmeric, ginger, cinnamon, and honey. Whisk well until combined.
3. Drink warm.
4. Ingredient tip: When selecting ginger and turmeric, opt for organic and bioavailable kinds, as opposed to the ones you get as a spice at the grocery store. Your body can much more easily absorb the bioavailable spices than store-bought spices.
5. Substitution tip: You can use unsweetened almond milk or oat milk as well, but in that case, add ¼ teaspoon of vanilla extract.

PER SERVING

Calories: 74.9 | Fat: 1.9g | Protein: 0.9g | Carbohydrates: 12.9g | Fiber: 1.9g | Sugar: 32.9g | Sodium: 107mg

Appendix 1 Index

A

agave nectar 39
almond butter 77
almond milk 40, 49
apple 14, 16, 21, 22, 26, 30, 33, 38, 50, 51, 56, 60, 62, 67, 68, 73, 75, 80, 85
apple cider 89
apple cider vinegar 67
apple juice 30, 53, 57
apples 58
apricots 37
artichoke heart 23
arugula 29, 72
asparagus 37
asparagus tips 35, 54
avocado 37, 57, 77, 88

B

baby greens mix 37
baby spinach leaves 42
banana 20, 34, 39, 40, 42, 43, 46, 47, 48, 49, 53, 56, 64, 72, 74, 77, 78, 87, 88, 94
basil leaves 27, 28, 80, 84
beet 30, 49, 55, 63, 65
beet with greens 16
blackberries 71
blueberries 50, 51, 53, 61, 64, 65, 69, 74, 77, 79, 98
Bok Choy 77
broccoli florets 14, 15, 23, 29, 48, 80, 82, 83
Brussels sprouts 33, 80, 83

C

cabbage 13, 32, 55, 82
cacao nibs 57
can crushed pineapple 42
canned sliced beets 89
canned yams in light syrup 89
cantaloupe 13, 37, 39, 42, 62, 63, 66, 82, 90
carrot 14, 16, 19, 34, 36, 49, 55, 56, 65, 77
carrot with greens 16, 20, 22, 23, 34, 54, 55, 56, 81, 83
cauliflower 80
celery 53, 57
celery stalk 16, 49, 77
Celery sticks 85
celery stocks 61, 66
chamomile flowers 62, 66
charcoal activated 62, 68
cherries 99
chia seeds 78, 85

chopped beet greens 26
chopped green onions 24
chopped mint 23
cilantro 60, 68
cinnamon 16, 50, 51, 100
cinnamon sticks 89
clementine 65
clove garlic 16, 23, 24, 25, 55, 77, 82, 84
cocoa powder 17
coconut milk 39
collard green 62, 68
cranberries 18, 20, 38, 81
cucumber 14, 19, 20, 21, 22, 23, 24, 26, 28, 29, 30, 33, 34, 37, 47, 48, 49, 53, 54, 55, 56, 60, 62, 68, 73, 75, 77, 78, 79, 80, 82, 83, 90, 91, 99

D

dates 71
diet blueberry-pomegranate juice 98

F

fat-free (skim) milk 92, 95, 96, 98
fat-free peach yogurt 40
Fennel 35
fennel bulb 80
fennel greens 36
flaxseed 63
fresh and frozen fruit 38
fresh baby spinach 49
fresh peaches 39
frozen berries 43
frozen blackberries 71
frozen blueberries 47, 71
frozen peach slices 47
frozen pineapple chunks 39, 73
frozen strawberries 46, 47

G

ginger 18, 20, 21, 22, 62, 63, 65, 66, 68, 74, 84
ginger root 64
granular sucralose sweetener (such as Splenda) 44
grape flavored sports drink 45
grape tomatoes 61, 66
grapefruit 18
grapes 38
Greek yogurt 57, 65
Greek yogurt vanilla or coconut flavor 39
green apple 13, 19, 29, 54
green bell pepper 14, 16, 28, 34, 83, 84
green grapes 48
green tea 65, 74

Smoothie for Weight Loss | 101

green tea with mandarin orange flavor tea bags 87
ground cardamom 17, 71
ground cinnamon 17, 46, 89
ground cloves 17
ground ginger 46, 100
ground nutmeg 17
ground turmeric 73

H
head cabbage 14, 16
honey 40, 43, 57, 61, 89, 98, 100
honeydew 79
honeydew melon 42, 48
hot sauce 53, 57

I
Ice cube trays 93

J
jalapeño pepper 19, 27, 35
jasmine green tea 58
juice 60

K
kale 36, 50, 51, 57, 60, 68, 73, 75, 77, 85
kiwis 13, 21, 29, 32, 53, 74, 84, 95

L
leafy greens 38
leaves of mint 60, 67
lemon 15, 18, 19, 22, 24, 28, 32, 35, 37, 42, 60, 61, 62, 63, 66, 67, 68, 69, 81, 90, 93
lemon juice 64, 73, 75, 85, 89, 92, 97
light chocolate syrup 87
lime 13, 42, 60, 68, 71, 83, 91, 99
lime juice 88
low-fat milk 40
low-sugar orange juice drink 88

M
mâché salad 74
mango 36, 44, 57, 63, 78, 85, 88
maple syrup 27
maqui berry powder 66
milk 45, 47, 93, 97
mint leaves 20, 54, 84
mixed berries 60, 67, 89, 91

N
nondairy or dairy milk 71, 72, 73
no-sugar-added orange juice 89
nutmeg 50, 51
nuts 72

O
orange 18, 24, 40, 42, 56, 80, 81

orange juice 43, 44, 48, 49, 50
orange juice concentrate 96
oregano leaves 33

P
paper 92, 94, 95, 97, 98
parsley 85
pear 36, 62, 63, 66, 72
pineapple 21, 74, 78, 85
plain non-fat Greek yogurt 90, 93, 97
plain non-fat yogurt 92
plain yogurt 43, 44
plastic cups 92, 94, 95, 97, 98
plum 13, 84
pomegranate seed 78
pop molds 92, 97
Pop molds with lids 96
pop sticks 92, 94, 95, 97
protein powder 56
pumpkin puree 46

R
raspberries 13, 27, 40, 97
raspberry sherbet 98
red bell pepper 37, 77
red grapes 65
red seedless grapes 46
reduced-fat (2%) milk 87
rhubarb 36
Roma tomato 27
romaine lettuce 29, 60, 68, 77

S
salt 44, 72, 88
sea beans 61, 66
seedless green grapes 51
seeds 72
sour cherries 21
spinach 13, 15, 16, 19, 20, 25, 30, 33, 34, 37, 38, 40, 43, 50, 51, 54, 56, 60, 65, 68, 72, 73, 75, 80, 82, 83, 84, 99
spirulina 37
sprig parsley 15
sprigs cilantro 19
sprigs dill 28
stalks celery 14, 15, 21, 24, 27, 30, 33, 34, 35, 82
stevia 17, 39, 51, 67
strawberries 32, 36, 39, 40, 43, 48, 49, 50, 53, 58, 65, 78, 79, 88, 90, 92, 94, 95
strawberry-flavor low-fat yogurt 95
strong brewed coffee 87
sugar 42, 87, 90, 91, 92, 93, 97
sugar-free maple syrup 89
sweetener 39, 61, 69, 72
sweet potato 18, 55, 82

Swiss Chard 35, 36, 74

T

tomato 15, 16, 24, 25, 27, 28, 29, 30, 32, 33, 37, 39, 53, 57, 77, 84
tomato juice 53, 57
Truvia natural sweetener 49
turmeric 100

U

unsweetened almond milk 17
unsweetened applesauce 46
unsweetened cranberry juice 64
unsweetened plain almond milk 94
unsweetened rice milk 27
unsweetened vanilla almond milk 100

V

vanilla 27, 88, 96
vanilla almond milk 57
vanilla extract 44, 50, 51, 71
vanilla ice cream 45
vanilla low-fat yogurt 88, 96
vanilla yogurt 47

W

watercress 72
watermelon 40, 45, 79
wheatgrass 18, 63
whey protein powder, vanilla 40
white potato 82
white sugar 44, 45, 48

Y

yellow beet 34, 81
yogurt 46

Z

zucchini 24, 25, 28, 44, 61, 66

Appendix 2 Measurement Conversion Chart

Volume Equivalents (Dry)	
US STANDARD	METRIC (APPROXIMATE)
1/8 teaspoon	0.5 mL
1/4 teaspoon	1 mL
1/2 teaspoon	2 mL
3/4 teaspoon	4 mL
1 teaspoon	5 mL
1 tablespoon	15 mL
1/4 cup	59 mL
1/2 cup	118 mL
3/4 cup	177 mL
1 cup	235 mL
2 cups	475 mL
3 cups	700 mL
4 cups	1 L

Volume Equivalents (Liquid)		
US STANDARD	US STANDARD (OUNCES)	METRIC (APPROXIMATE)
2 tablespoons	1 fl.oz.	30 mL
1/4 cup	2 fl.oz.	60 mL
1/2 cup	4 fl.oz.	120 mL
1 cup	8 fl.oz.	240 mL
1 1/2 cup	12 fl.oz.	355 mL
2 cups or 1 pint	16 fl.oz.	475 mL
4 cups or 1 quart	32 fl.oz.	1 L
1 gallon	128 fl.oz.	4 L

Temperatures Equivalents	
FAHRENHEIT(F)	CELSIUS(C) APPROXIMATE)
225 °F	107 °C
250 °F	120 ° °C
275 °F	135 °C
300 °F	150 °C
325 °F	160 °C
350 °F	180 °C
375 °F	190 °C
400 °F	205 °C
425 °F	220 °C
450 °F	235 °C
475 °F	245 °C
500 °F	260 °C

Weight Equivalents	
US STANDARD	METRIC (APPROXIMATE)
1 ounce	28 g
2 ounces	57 g
5 ounces	142 g
10 ounces	284 g
15 ounces	425 g
16 ounces (1 pound)	455 g
1.5 pounds	680 g
2 pounds	907 g

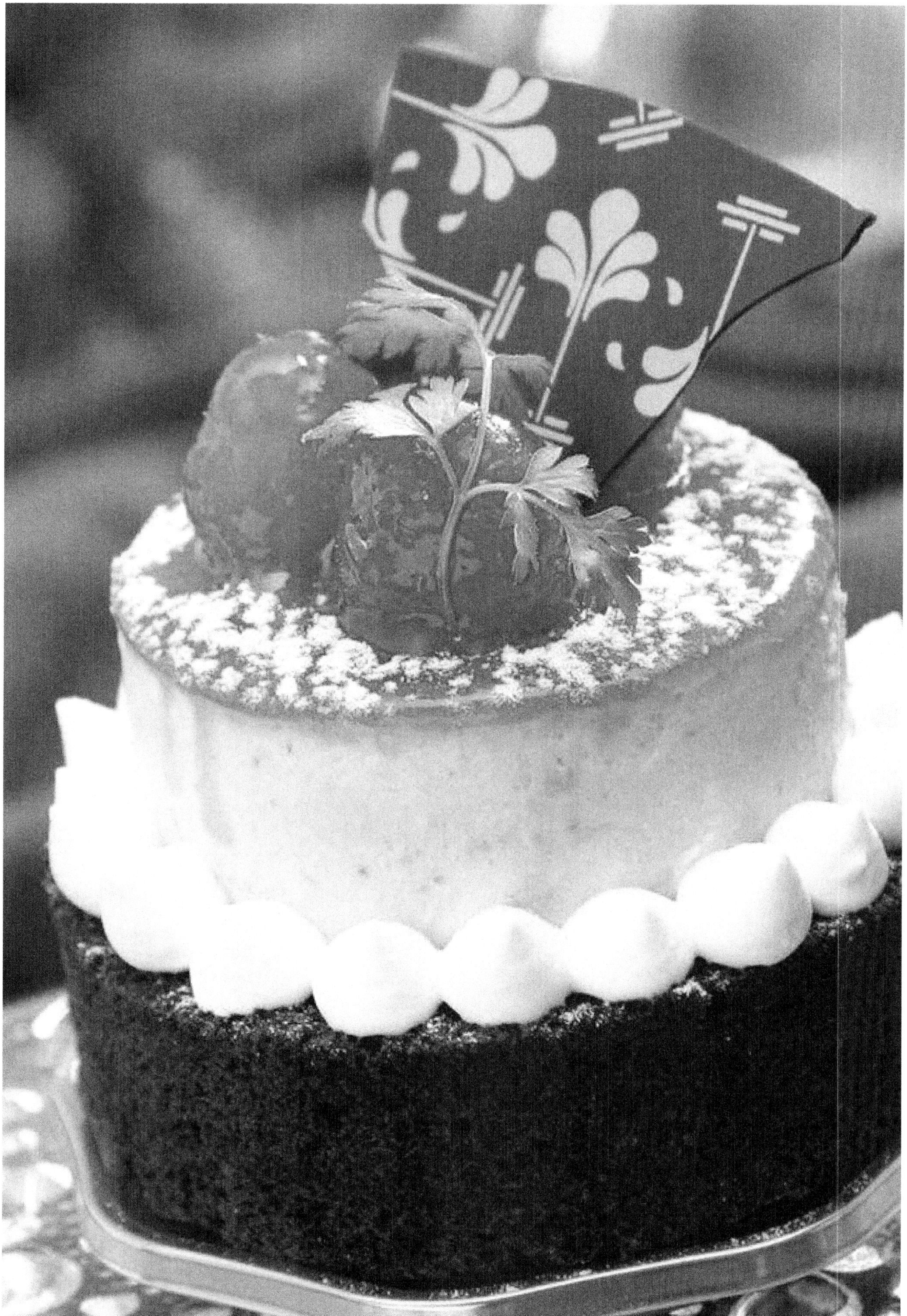

DORIS M. SMITH

Printed in Great Britain
by Amazon